D1052784

Woman to Woman

Woman to Woman

Handing on Our Experiences of the Joyful, Sorrowful, and Glorious Mysteries of Life

by Ronda Chervin, Terri Vorndran Nichols,
and the Marian Women in Ministry

Ignatius Press   San Francisco

Book design by Darlene S. O'Rourke
Cover design by Riz Boncan Marsella
Cover illustration by Anne Dobbins
Text illustrations by Marcia Ryan

Published with ecclesiastical approval
The granting of the *Imprimatur*
does not imply the acceptance of the
theological opinions of the author.
© 1988 Ignatius Press, San Francisco
All rights reserved
ISBN 0–89870–182–1 (SB)
ISBN 0–89870–264–x (HB)
Library of Congress catalogue number 88–80659
Printed in the United States of America

Woman to Woman is a book of reflections, meditations, and readings primarily for women, about women, by women. It is a guide to living in modern times while retaining our faith, hope, charity, sanity, and sense of humor!

We dedicate this book for women to the most perfect of all women, Mary, the Mother of our Lord, to whom we look for comfort, strength, guidance and closeness to her Son.

This book was written "that others may take courage from the insights that have helped me along the road" (Ronda); and "in tribute to the saints that fascinate me, and in kinship with women everywhere who share my faith" (Terri). The Marian Women in Ministry is a network of women who love Jesus in the Church and claim Mary as their Mother.

Contents

Preface 9

THE JOYFUL MYSTERIES
OF BEING A WOMAN

Womanly Joy 13
Falling in Love 15
Marriage 19
Motherhood 24
On Being a Single Woman 37
On Being a Consecrated Woman 50
Enjoying Our Feminine Traits 61
The Joyful Mysteries of the Rosary 98

THE SORROWFUL MYSTERIES
OF BEING A WOMAN

Womanly Suffering 101
The Sufferings of the Body 104
The Sufferings of the Heart 115
Healing Our Feminine Faults 147
The Sorrowful Mysteries of the Rosary 175

Woman to Woman

THE GLORIOUS MYSTERIES OF BEING
A WOMAN OF THE CHURCH

On Being a Woman of the Church 179
The Sacraments of the Church 180
The Prayer of the Church 189
Women in Ministry 203
Catholic Faith, Hope, and Love 209
The Glorious Mysteries of the Rosary 255

Afterword 257
Bibliography 259
Index 265

Preface

Woman to Woman comes out of an experience I am sure many of you share. Accustomed to being taught primarily by men about how to lead a Catholic Christian life, I still often feel a great need for the wisdom of other women. This is because I know that another woman has gone through a lot of the same problems I have suffered through and also enjoyed some of the same happiness.

Many times when giving workshops designed for a feminine audience I have been told that the insights given have been deeply helpful. And usually some of the women attending will find time to tell me how they have found Christ on their journeys. Their stories have greatly enriched me.

Three years ago, I was chosen as one of five women consultants to the United States Bishops writing a Pastoral on the Concerns of Women. During this process, with its many national hearings and reports from local diocesan groups, I had occasion to listen to the voices of many women who feel bitterly disappointed in our Church. Some of these women openly dissent from Catholic teaching, and some defy Church discipline in a spirit of protest. I also heard from many women who, though wanting to see some changes, basically love the Church. These women often feel isolated.

As a response to these voices, I organized a group called Marian Women in Ministry to serve as a network for women who find strength from the perennial spirituality of the Catholic Church and who are grateful to have Mary as their Mother and the women saints as their models. I distribute a monthly letter to these women, including my own thoughts and favorite quotations, as well as their sharings. The letter has met with such a favorable response that I was inspired to put together a book for many Christian women to read and to give to their friends and relatives.

I asked my dear friend Terri Vorndran Nichols, also a writer, to contribute short lives of women saints and also to write the section on faith. Unless otherwise noted, the biographies of the saints included here are written by Terri.

In honor of our Lady, I chose the themes of the joyful, sorrowful, and glorious mysteries of women. May God increase the faith, hope, and love of all who read *Woman to Woman*.

Ronda Chervin

The

Joyful Mysteries

Of Being a Woman

Womanly Joy

The truth and light of the soul is nothing else but God. I beg you to be full of gaiety. Oh! how much it is needed by people of good will. This gaiety is willed by God. We ought to honor it in the Heart of the Lord and strive to draw it to ourselves.

Anon.

There is rapture dwelling essentially in all experience.

Pieper

We die daily. Happy those who daily come to life as well.

MacDonald

In the lines of these favorite quotations, I would like to intersperse the word "womanly". "I beg you to be full of womanly gaiety", "there is rapture in all feminine experience", "happy those women who daily come to life as well."

So many women today seem to hate being women, so great are the burdens and conflicts. Yet when asked at workshops about their womanhood, most women would not like to be men instead. Asked what they like best about being women, many speak about being able to express their feelings.

We love to overflow with positive feelings—of love, of delight, of adoration of God. For me, such moments

13

are connected with falling in love, with the sight of newborn babies and the enjoyment of their early days of life, with deep inner prayer and with communal prayer and praise, with love of nature, and with special times of expressing love to family and friends.

You might write up your own most joyful moments of being a woman and let feelings of the past well up in you again, thanking God for them.

In the joyful mysteries of being a woman, I have included sharings about falling in love, marriage, children, the single life, the consecrated life, and particular feminine ways that bring joy, such as love of beauty, sweetness, simplicity, nesting, heart-to-heart friendship.

Lest this section seem too rosy, I promise you that the next one about the sorrowful mysteries of women will be the same length.

Falling in Love

Let him kiss me with the kisses of his mouth!
More delightful is your love than wine!

Ah, you are beautiful, my beloved,
   ah, you are beautiful. . . .

Hark! my lover—here he comes
   springing across the mountains,
   leaping across the hills.

My lover speaks; he says to me,
"Arise my beloved, my beautiful one, and come!
For see, the winter is past,
   the rains are over and gone.
The flowers appear on the earth,
   the time of pruning the vines has come,
   and the song of the dove is heard in our land.[1]

One of the happiest times of my life was my courtship
with my husband-to-be. This followed a long stream of
miserable relationships. The sorrowful side of love will
be described in the next section, but for now let us rejoice
in our memories and present experiences of joyful falling
in love and marital union.

Falling in love is one of the ways we come to appreciate
God's love, for we join the stream of love that God has

[1] The Song of Songs 1:2, 15; 2:8, 10–12.

for the beloved. Fascinated, we see the true beauty of a human person. Our love says Amen to God's creation. And this delight takes place even when love is not requited or is destined to be overcome by obstacles we cannot control.

When this love is returned, we feel ecstatic. In the mirror of the eyes of the lover we see ourselves as beautiful, and we are healed, for a while at least, of the horrible interiorized images of self we read in the eyes of those who did not appreciate us.

Love is a foretaste of heaven, for there we will know an integration of body, heart, mind, and spirit such as we glimpse when our eyes, with intense wonder, meet those of the one we love.

Strangely enough, human love, as beautiful and glorious as it is, cannot be sustained by human beings! It is destined to dwindle unless it is renewed by the redemptive graces of Christ.

To think that human love alone can make us totally happy, as those who have just fallen in love tend to believe, is an illusion which seems harmless enough at the time. But it is really a danger, because it places a terrible burden on imperfect people to give perfect fulfillment to each other.

The more we make an idol of the absolute happiness-giving powers of the one who loves us, the more disappointed we are bound to become. Instead of moving toward idol worship, the Christian woman should place God's love in the center of her life as the absolute source of joy. We should be delighted with our loved ones and grateful for the happiness they bring, but not overly dependent. To build the kingdom of love on earth as it is in heaven means forming many friendships, not hiding two by two in desperation.

To conclude, here are some prayer exercises to examine our human love and help center this love in Christ:

1. Meditate on your experiences of falling in love and thank God for this great blessing. Meditate on heaven as an eternity of such happiness.

2. Fall in love with Jesus by thinking of his goodness, beauty, and holiness. Let his love for you as a unique person created by God and redeemed by his blood fill your heart.

3. If you are not sure whether you are in love or not, consider the characteristics of love mentioned in this chapter in the form of these questions: a. Do I feel really happy in the presence of the one I think I love or only when thinking about my beloved in his absence? b. Do I feel myself to be lovable when I am with the one who claims to love me, or do I mainly feel confused or that I am being loved only for external reasons? c. Does this love make me feel whole, or do I feel a conflict between thoughts, feelings, and hopes? For example, do I feel distress when I think about his personality and only feel happy during physical contact? Do I feel happy thinking about him but actually restless and critical and unable to be natural when I am in his presence?

4. To appraise whether you are ready to marry someone you love, think prayerfully about these factors: a. Are the negative qualities in each of us gradually changing for the better, or are they becoming intensified? b. Do we have a source of strength outside of ourselves in God's grace, or do we reach an insuperable limit when we come into conflict—which conflict is settled only by a rush of passing feeling which soon dissolves? c. Have I given this

love time to pass through many "seasons" so that I can see if the obstacles in life are stronger than my love for him? For example, does my desire to marry really depend on a certain image of the future based on his going into a certain occupation so that we could have a certain kind of life together? Do I find that I just can't put up with his faults or he with mine? Do we find that we can help each other, or do we always go to others for help, being close to each other only when we can show our "best selves"?

Marriage

The sum which two married people owe to one another
defies calculation. It is an infinite debt, which can only be
discharged through all eternity.

Goethe

God did not create woman from man's head that he shall
command her; nor from his feet that she should be his
slave, but rather from his side, that she should be near his
heart.

The Talmud

And they shall be two in one flesh.

Mark 10:6–8

Marriage is a wonderful vocation. What many have
discovered, to their surprise, is that there can be a deep
renewal of the joy of falling in love later on in a marriage
after it has passed through many trials and even seemed
to be dead. Here are two favorite quotations on this
subject:

The whole aim of marriage is to fight through and survive
the instant when incompatibility becomes unquestionable.
For a man and a woman, as such, are incompatible.

G. K. Chesterton

Marriage is a closed society. You invent your own myth-
ology and language. That is why I tend to be against

divorce. You can't snuff out an entire civilization like that, by an act of will. All marriages are miserable. They have to be. But you've got to push on with it, because it's a civilization . . . a handing down of shorthands, special gestures, and vocabularies which stand for a whole complexity that you have to be very glad to be able to express.

Anthony Burgess

Here are a few poems I have written about marriage to share with you my perception of its mysteries:

At the hour when
dark seems stronger than light
and uncertainty clutches the heart,
we fumble for each other,
unite,
then sleep in peace,
knowing once again that
"love is stronger than death".

Some days we are like
two parallel rails on a track
going from time to eternity.
The children ride heavily over us.
Occasionally a gleam of light
bounces from your track to mine
or mine to yours;
we are together, but do not touch,
and yet our love is dear.

Marriage:
bright, sour peel
sweet, tasty pulp
bruised, brown dents
tough, inner core
lovely, smooth seeds.

Some of the most important ideas about the sacrament of marriage come from two famous Catholic philosophers whose writings I have studied in detail: Dietrich von Hildebrand and Karol Wojtyla (John Paul II).[1]

The Holy Father's thoughts about marriage spring from his great sense of wonder at the glory of the creation of the two sexes. John Paul II came from a very loving family. A crucial aspect of his work for the Church is in recreating for others the vision of marriage which corresponds to God's will for the human family.

In the Pope's philosophy, sex is for the purpose of expressing fruitful love through the body to recover the original unity of Adam and Eve. We should not think of others in terms of how we can use them for our own pleasure or even to satisfy our need for mutual affection. True love, instead, is a commitment to the happiness of the other.

To be in the image and likeness of God means primarily to be able to love. Marital love involves an "all-encompassing self-surrender for the sake of the other. When a married couple acts in accordance with their vows and God's will, they are a sign (a sacrament), a physical manifestation, of the lover of persons."[2] This is why marriage is indissoluble, and the family is a miniature domestic church.

Von Hildebrand, whose writings influenced the Pope, wrote of the high degree of union between spouses that

[1] See Dietrich von Hildebrand's book, *Marriage* (Sophia Press, 1984) and Karol Wojtyla's book, *Covenant of Love* (Doubleday, 1986) which summarize much of their thought on marriage.

[2] From John Paul II, *Familiaris Consortio*. Also see *Covenant of Love*.

comes with mutual self-surrender in light of the unique preciousness of the beloved which each responds to totally. Von Hildebrand, in *Marriage*, explains why marriage needs the completion of a vow to be fulfilled:

> But conjugal love is not yet marriage, although it contains an anticipation of the meaning of marriage. Marriage is a reality in the objective order which is constituted only by a solemn act and presupposes a formal act of the will: the two partners give themselves expressly to each other, fully sanctioning this surrender for their entire lifetime. The marriage is fully actualized when both partners, in consequence of this act, consummate this surrender in bodily union. Marriage is a communion of objective validity, including both partners and, once established, persists as such regardless of the sentiments or attitudes of the partners, although it imposes specific obligations on them.
>
> The existence of conjugal love between the partners makes marriage desirable and gives it meaning, but does not in itself establish this objective bond. Among the various human experiences there is one kind which is not merely an inner act in respect to another person such as love, respect, joy, and so on, but which *creates* an *objective reality* independent of the person. Thus a promise creates an obligation toward another person and the right of demanding fulfillment by that other person.[3]

Even in the case of an unhappy marriage, God will bless the love that is given day by day in the spirit of self-sacrifice. We should call upon the graces of the sacrament throughout our married lives.

[3] *Marriage*, p. 17ff.

Pat McAuley, a Marian Woman in Ministry, writes that she has

> become increasingly aware of the differences in the lives (particularly in the marriage relationship and in how the children are doing) of those of us who do and do not realize that the teachings of the Church are a manifestation of Christ's incredible love for us poor fallen children. There just are not enough mountain tops from which to shout this.

Motherhood

Every child comes with the message that God is not yet discouraged of man.

Tagore

First give them roots; then give them wings.

Anon.

The beauty of a creature is nothing but the likeness of divine beauty participated in things.

Thomas Aquinas

The most important person on earth is a mother. She cannot claim the honor of having built Notre Dame Cathedral. She need not. She has built something more magnificent than any cathedral—a dwelling for an immortal soul, the tiny perfection of her baby's body. . . . The angels have not been blessed with such a grace. They cannot share in God's creative miracle to bring new saints to heaven. Only a human mother can. Mothers are closer to God the Creator than any other creatures. God joins forces with mothers in performing this act of creation. . . . What on God's earth is more glorious than this: *to be a mother*?

Joseph Cardinal Mindszenty

Many are my own joys in being a mother. It is many years since my pregnancies, but they were dramatic enough with twins coming first, then three miscarriages, a son, and three more miscarriages.

Having no knowledge of babies, and ideas of childbirth right out of nineteenth century novels, I was quite apprehensive about my first pregnancy until I started taking a natural childbirth class. My first full sense of joy came when I was told to go to a hospital before my own childbirth to view the little newborns. I experienced an ecstatic affection for those tiny bundles and great fantasies about my forthcoming child. I didn't find out until delivery that I had twins. My happiness in encountering the personalities of my babies was overwhelming. It was for me a very contemplative experience to gaze into their soulful eyes. Of course that bliss ended abruptly when they came into their two-fold terrible twos.

At the time of my twins' birth twenty-three years ago, breastfeeding was not encouraged. Three miscarriages later, with other sorrows in between, I found that nursing my miraculously surviving son was one of the most delightful times of my life. How grateful I am to La Leche friends who urged me to persist in nursing the baby even though he was a preemie and unable to suck for awhile.

As one who dislikes sensory-related tasks and who is also irritable in the extreme, I found raising children to be the most difficult task I have ever tried. And yet, in a million years I would never exchange a child for a career or prefer to write a book over having a baby. A human being is eternally precious, a career or a book is just for time.

In later years, what I love best about being a mother is the intimacy I feel toward my children, the closeness even after conflict. I also love the beauty of their faces and forms and their accomplishments in art, poetry, music, writing. I love to see them giving love in abundance to those in need.

Now, about to be a grandmother for the first time, I wrote a few lines in honor of the phases I have passed through:

♥♥　　girl heart,
　　　eager, adoring

　　　mother heart,
　　　tender, troubled

　　　middle-aged heart,
　　　passionate, bitter

　　　grandmother heart,
　　　large, soft.　　　♥♥

Here are some other contributions about motherhood and children:

> The most joyful experience to me as a woman is the moment in your life when you hold innocence itself in your arms and caress its untarnished beauty. This radiant innocence is held for only moments before it takes on worldly wise ways and is taken from you. This wide-eyed and beautiful innocence is manifested in the spring of motherhood.
>
> Melinda Brogan

And John Pepping, one of the many men who like to receive our Marian Letter, writes:

> In all of God's beautiful, wonderful and reverence-inspiring creation, one thing stands out above all the others . . . a child. And the awesome fact is that this is the one thing that God and man create together.

If anyone should ever ask you for a definition of love, just say a child. For a child is born of love; needs love to subsist; and brings love into the lives of all around him. *No* one needs more love than a child. *No* one gives more love than a child. When a home is filled with children, the home is full of love. That is why there is nothing among all the beautiful, wonderful, marvelous things in God's universe that can compare to one innocent child.

ELIZABETH BAYLEY SETON

The year was 1774, two years before ink was penned on the Declaration of Independence. An American flag was close to waving with a circle of thirteen stars, fife and drum was in the air, and three-cornered hats covered some of the boldest minds in history: Paul Revere, George Washington, Thomas Jefferson. . . .

The first Continental Congress, a gathering of leaders from Great Britain's thirteen American colonies, met in Philadelphia on August 28, 1774. This was the first united stand taken by the Colonies against the mother country and was to lead to the War of Independence and the birth of the United States of America. Six days before that decisive pivot in history, a child was born named Elizabeth Bayley. The Revolution swirling

We encourage you to read a full biography of our remarkable American saint and patroness of motherhood (see bibliography).

around the little girl became a fitting backdrop for the pioneering course of her own important life. For while Richard Bayley, Elizabeth's physician father, was a loyalist who clung to the British crown, she herself—later to be Mother Seton—apparently assimilated the daring of her times. She converted to Catholicism despite family shock, founded parochial schools as we know them today, and became the very first American-born saint to be canonized.

Elizabeth Bayley was a true daughter of the American Revolution. The year of her birth saw the battles of Lexington and Concord. At age nine she watched the redcoats being marched out of New York City and the hoisting of the Stars and Stripes. At fifteen, she quite possibly witnessed the inauguration of George Washington. Patriotic determination and freedom were the jewels of the new republic. In Elizabeth Bayley Seton the gifts of her era were spiritualized and transformed into great holiness.

Mother Seton's life is rich with hope for all women because, one by one, she embraced the gamut of our callings: daughter, wife, lover, friend, orphan, widow, mother, neighbor, patriot, convert, teacher, leader, and religious.

She also experienced our roller coaster of joys and grief. Her eight-year marriage to William Seton was joyously alive with love and intimacy, and their five children filled her with pleasure. But she equally received her lion's share of hard luck and heartache. She lost people she loved. Her mother died when she was three. And one by one it happened to others she cherished: father, beloved husband, four of her five children, and other close relatives and friends. Moreover, her Protestant relatives ostracized her once she became a Catholic.

In childhood, after her mother died, Elizabeth was doubly vulnerable because the woman her father remarried never warmed her with any affection. Elizabeth was a sensitive child who longed to give and receive love. During long visits to her Uncle William's New Rochelle farm, a 250-acre shorefront ranch overlooking Long Island Sound, she and her sister basked in the companionship of their cousins. It was there that Elizabeth started loving God, coming close to him through the quiet beauty of nature. She once said of the sea, the sky, the flowers and foliage, and the colors of the seasons: "They each remind me in some way of God." When she was old enough to read, Elizabeth found consolation from Scripture, especially the Psalms, and the *Imitation of Christ*. Those two books would be her lifelong companions.

Time away from her father, though, was excruciating. As a brilliant physician who traveled extensively, he had little time for the daughters from his first marriage. Yet he was one of the persons who inspired Elizabeth to become such a saintly woman. One summer after her father became New York's First Health Officer, she visited him on Staten Island at the quarantine hospital where he gave himself freely to hundreds of impoverished, disease-ridden immigrants. A grace touched Elizabeth's soul that summer as she watched her father's Christ-like, almost heroic charity. She was equally impressed with the acceptance and confidence in God that she found on the part of the suffering foreigners. America's future first Sister of Charity learned priceless strategies of courage and love at that early quarantine hospital on Staten Island. The lessons steeled her through many crosses, including her father's death once he caught the yellow fever.

Beautiful in body as well as soul, and very charming, Elizabeth captured the attention of many men. She eventually chose to marry William Magee Seton, a handsome, well-off young businessman with whom she loved to dance and go to the theater. When she was eighteen and he was twenty-four they married, loving each other intensely. Mother Seton seems to be the perfect patron of happy marriages because her life in that arena was so balanced and fulfilling. Initially the couple lived on Stone Street with the groom's father and motherless brothers and sisters. The incorporation of the Setons' young, happy marriage into that wider household of people who adored Elizabeth, asked her advice, and showered her with affection, seemed to be a pledge from God to Elizabeth that he had read all her secret dreams and made them come true. The marriage was also enriched with five children, and here again Elizabeth was full of merriment and happiness. She once told someone, "My precious children stick to me like little burrs . . . the moment I shake one off one side, the other clings in the opposite." Anna Maria, Rebecca, Bill, Dick, and little Kit brought William and Elizabeth even closer and more tenderly together.

Sorrow punctured Elizabeth's life again, however, when her husband's lucrative shipping business collapsed from piracy on the open seas. That in itself Elizabeth could handle. On December 7, 1800, she wrote to her close friend Julia Scott:

> The winder up of our bankrupts sits in our library, taking inventory of our furniture, goods, etc. . . . and yet Seton is writing quietly by my side, in as perfect health as he has ever enjoyed. My chicks are quiet in bed. For myself, I think the greatest happiness of this life is to be released from the cares and formalities of what is called the world. My world is my family, and the only change for me will be that I can devote myself unmolested to my treasure. . . . When the clouds seem to hang heaviest I trust where my trust has never yet failed.

Poverty was not frightening to Elizabeth Seton, but something else gradually came to be: her husband's decline in health became a threatening shadow over her gloriously rich marriage and family life. In October of 1803 Elizabeth agreed to take her sick husband and their eight-year-old daughter Anna to Leghorn, Italy, where some kind, old business friends had offered their aid. The Filicchis eagerly awaited the reunion on November 18, but when William disembarked from the *Shepherdess* he was inspected, jostled around, and ordered to the quarantine. The yellow fever plague in New York was making all of Europe nervous.

What happened at the Leghorn quarantine makes me love Elizabeth Seton, because she clearly was one of the kindest and strongest women of her day. The Leghorn quarantine, first of all, was on a canal several miles from the city. The family was rowed out to the dungeon-like building and motioned up a long flight of stairs to Room No. 6. Seton could barely walk by this point, but the boatmen ran away for fear of catching the disease. Elizabeth managed to take her husband up the stairs, love and comfort him in a dank, little cell stripped of goods, and equally attend to little Anna who was cold, confused and frightened. One of the sweetest touches of Elizabeth's kindness at this time was the way that she played with Anna, jumping rope together and holding her while she sang softly or spoke with her. This image of Elizabeth—gentle and strong —is the one that emerges in all of her ordeals. It must have been the mother in her. Of all the saints, she is one of the most feminine.

Luckily, the Filicchi family was able to get the quarantine lifted ten days ahead of schedule. In the beautiful lodging reserved for them by the Filicchis, William died quietly in God's grace. "For three days and three nights", Elizabeth wrote, "the fatigue was incessant. I had done all that the tenderest love and the duty of a wife could do."

Elizabeth Seton was widowed at twenty-nine. She was a penniless mother of five, but often in adversities God plants the seeds of opportunity. Elizabeth was on European soil far from home surrounded by a loving family of devout Catholics. The sweet, devotional comforts and the liturgical majesty of the Faith started opening Elizabeth's eyes. When Anthony Filicchi accompanied Elizabeth and Anna back to New York, they spent many hours on the sea voyage talking about God and spiritual things. By the time Elizabeth set foot in New York harbor, she was already a Catholic in her heart.

The decision cost her the love and help of her Episcopalian relatives. People in New York just did not become Catholic. The poor Irish immigrants, for example, were a rejected, unacceptable breed. Interestingly, these were the very people that Elizabeth's father had treated on Staten Island. She remembered his love for them, and felt in God's presence when near them. Weighing the price, Elizabeth chose the Faith. There really was no contest. She had discovered the Real Presence in the Eucharist and the other sacraments. There was no turning back.

In 1806, a Father Dubourg approached Elizabeth Seton with the comment that there was not one Catholic girls' school in the United States. Their discussion bore rich and historical fruit when Elizabeth Seton set up her own little school in Baltimore. Her first assistant was Cecilia O'Conway from Philadelphia, who had desired a religious life in Europe since there was no religious novitiate in the United States. Others like Cecilia came, including a widow like Elizabeth, who had hoped for a religious community life after her husband's death. With these Catholic teachers in charge the school soon filled with children from all over the neighborhood and provinces beyond.

Eventually a kind aspirant to the priesthood offered Elizabeth ten thousand dollars to establish a bigger house for the teaching of orphan children. Providentially, a fifty acre farm was purchased close to the village of Emmitsburg, fifty miles west of Baltimore. Before moving to that location permanently, Elizabeth took private vows before Archbishop John Carroll. She was the first Sister of Charity and the foundress of a whole community of Sisters that thrives to this day.

Those early Sisters of Charity were pioneers of formal Catholic education. They were also the first native religious community. Although Mother Seton was very humble and engaging to men of the cloth with outside advice, she was firm in defending the autonomy of her community since she believed that some of the priests did know how to deal with women as she did.

In spite of the success of this undertaking, Mother Seton suffered aggravations and sorrows, just as in the early years of her life. God seemed to create in Elizabeth, with grace and her cooperation, a strong, calm center. However, she never became accustomed to the crushing spiritual pains associated with losing a loved one. Even as Mother Seton extended maternal love to a wider and wider circle of children, four of her own children became gravely sick and died. Illustrating how motherly and almost girlish a part of her remained, Elizabeth wrote to her generous friend Julia Scott on February 16, 1816:

> A thought struck me. My darling daughter Rebecca has a particular delight in dolls, and as you have so long treated us all as pets, I do imagine it may be a particular pleasure for you to send us one, along with the little articles of dress. Do you think I would ask you so expressive a thing without a reason? The fact is, Rebecca's health is weakening and her efforts to stay lively and courageous sometimes fail. Mother and a doll seem to be her only pleasure in life. . . . Kind Mrs. Chatard sent us a large, beautiful doll from Baltimore, but because it was wax it was quite broken up before it reached us.

The spirit of sensitivity to her daughter, and all her children and students, was a type of charism that Mother Seton gave to her fellow sisters. The thousands of Sisters of Charity that carry her legacy today run hospitals, nursing schools, colleges, grade and high schools, orphanages, and homes for the aged and the retarded.

When Elizabeth Seton was canonized on September 14, 1975, many must have seen that her life was like a beautiful tapestry in which the disappointments and obstacles stood out in colors and textures that make it unforgettable. Something that makes her a saint for our own challenging lives is that she found a way to thread the bright ribbons of hope and love all through it.

One of her letters to Julia Scott is one she might send to us today:

> Our God is God. All is as he pleases. I am the happiest creature in the thought that not the least thing can happen but by his will or permission; and all for the best. Our God! Echo it back, dearest one. Our God! and love your . . . Betsey Seton

Let me conclude this chapter on the joyful mystery of motherhood with prayers to Mary, our Mother in the Church, asking for her motherly intercession and guidance in our motherhood.

The Memorare

Remember, O most gracious Virgin Mary,
That never was it known
That anyone who fled to thy protection,
Implored thy help,
or sought thine intercession was left unaided.
Inspired by this confidence,
I fly to you, O Virgin of virgins, my Mother,
To thee do I come
before thee I stand, sinful and sorrowful.
O Mother of the Word Incarnate,
Despise not my petitions,
but in thy mercy,
hear and answer me. Amen.

Act of Consecration

My Queen, my Mother, I give myself entirely to you and to show my devotion to you, I consecrate to you this day my eyes, my ears, my mouth, my heart, my whole being without reserve! Wherefore, good Mother, as I am thine own, keep me, guard me, as thy property and possession. Amen.

On Being a
Single Woman

And the unmarried woman or girl is anxious about the affairs of the Lord, how to be holy in body and spirit. . . .[1]

Much is written about the sorrows of being a single woman. Here we want to focus on the joyful mysteries of this state. Freedom from encumbrances of the married and communal religious life is something that many single women find an attractive feature of their way of interacting with others. Some choose the single vocation because they seek solitude. Others remain single, but prefer the company of others and consider their times of solitude a cross of loneliness.

Dr. Susan Muto, director of the Institute for Formative Spirituality at Duquesne, wrote a beautiful book, *Celebrating the Single Life*, about the joys of this state, which she sees as chosen for us by God because of its special blessings of intimacy with the Lord.

A spirituality of the single life never makes singleness an end in itself, but sees it as a graced opportunity to orient one's life toward some kind of self-giving activity related to one's profession and position. This service may be public, but more often than not it is hidden. Active,

[1] I Corinthians 7:34.

dynamic single people usually lead a hidden life in the spiritual sense. While often being gifted, outgoing communicators, they need to retire in stillness. . . . Only in their diaries and letters do we learn of their being "spies for the Eternal", who conducted secret negotiations between God and man.[2]

Joy Bergman, a single contemplative woman and dear friend of mine, wrote a poem which suggests something about the single life, though it was not written for that purpose:

> The Holy Spirit
> It sings in my heart
> a wild bird
> and great
> Its wings flash
> across my soul

Kathy Hall, another favorite friend and an artist, wrote this about being a godmother:

Laura

Laura, since I'm Sarai without an Abraham
Your mother elected me to be your godmother.

I've a heavy responsibility to help you to heaven;
But when I touch you and you snuggle close,
    baby powder magic.

My breasts are dry of milk
But I will provide spiritual food.

I'll explain Kant
And educate your taste.

[2] *Celebrating the Single Life* (Doubleday, 1982), p. 46.

Tell me your secrets,
I'll protect you.

Your bright existence illuminates mine,
An old maid with her own godchild.

A quality that I find in many single women friends is
courage, the spunk to stand alone with the grace of
Christ and face the world as a self-chosen personality
without definition through family or community bonds.
One of my friends among Marian Women in Ministry
represents these qualities to an extraordinary degree as
this piece indicates:

CONFESSIONS OF
A PRO-LIFE SINGLE

by Juli Loesch

I don't know whether the human race will last another 500
years. But if we manage to avoid blowing ourselves away with
the Bomb, poisoning ourselves with toxic effluents, or erasing
our identities, line by line, with genetic engineering—that is to
say, if there exist on this planet, 500 years from now, human
beings who know they *are* human beings—those human beings
may well consider that they almost didn't make it. And they
may look back in history to ask themselves, "What was the
single most important event which saved the human project
on this planet—our human dignity—even, our human identity?
What was the turning point?"

I suggest that the turning point will have been this: the

Originally published in *Commonweal*, Oct. 18, 1985.

publication, in the Year of our Lord 1968, of the encyclical *Humanae Vitae*.

Well, *Humanae Vitae* wasn't any kind of turning point for *me*—certainly not at the time it was promulgated.

I graduated from the eighth grade in 1965, the closing year of Vatican II; and when *Humanae Vitae* came out, I was just entering my senior year of high school. If my grade school religious education featured a flashcard approach to doctrine, I must say that by my seventeenth birthday that deck had long since been tossed to the winds.

It was a hell of a year, anyhow, 1968. I was a single-issue fanatic against the war in Vietnam. I judged people (particularly *public* people) on this basis: are you opposed to the killing or are you not? There was the Tet Offensive in February of that year. Martin Luther King spoke out. King was murdered. Riots erupted. Bobby Kennedy triumphed in the California primary. Bobby was murdered. Allen Ginsberg celebrated the "Prague Spring" with flowers in his hair; then the Soviet tanks crushed all the flowers. Then there was the Democratic Convention Police Riot Extravaganza ("Welcome to Czechago") and I fell in love with Leo Tolstoy and the Jefferson Airplane and a young dissident named Thom who used to wear a long trailing scarf and looked just like Emmet Grogan. You know, the Digger. From San Francisco. And I went to dances and handed out leaflets against the draft.

All this set the stage for the way I accepted (read: didn't accept) *Humanae Vitae* at the time. The war had destroyed moral authority for us. What was there to believe in? . . .

Anyway, when *Humanae Vitae* came out, it wasn't hard to see which side I'd be on. I saw the charts that showed the growth rate of the human population shooting damn near vertically right off the page; . . . I read the comment of some smart dissident priestling to the effect that the new encyclical was "an intellectual embarrassment". (I liked smart dissidents.)

So, when early into the school year Sister Mary Claire

Kennedy asked me what did *I* think of *Humanae Vitae*, I threw
up my hands and pronounced in tones of exasperated common
sense "Aw, geez, Claire, if we don't have contraception, we
end up with abortion." Contraception was supposed to prevent abortion. It was possible to believe that, when you were
only seventeen, and it was 1968. "And besides," I opined
solemnly, "*Humanae Vitae* is an intellectual embarrassment."

Being young, healthy, and heterosexual, and being, within
the year, free of any adults with pretensions of governing me
in loco parentis, I was soon in an excellent position to experience
the personal and social benefits to be derived from sexuality
liberated from fertility.

At first, I fared pretty well. My "partner" (as the family
planning literature called him) was a genuinely good guy, and
I was carefree and pharmacologically infertile. I was vaguely
uneasy that I was putting chemicals into my body every day
that I'd hesitate to put into my compost pile. Then I read that
women with my kind of medical history who were on the Pill
could end up with a stroke.

I got off the Pill. I investigated other contraceptives. I drew a
garish diagram of my inner waterways with all the available
barriers and plugs, jellies and jams, and state-of-the-art devices
in place, and I was positively dismayed. Plastic domes, copper
shards, "Head 'em off at the Fallopian tubes!" "Poison gas
at the pass!" This wasn't Sexual Shalom—it was a cervical
Strategic Defense Initiative.

By 1972, the year before *Roe v. Wade*, about half my female
friends—at least, of those whom I knew well enough to know
such an intimate thing—had had abortions. A miserable fate
indeed.

So what was I to conclude? That females are a misbegotten
breed? That our bodies are basically, finally, not in our own
best interest?

No way. I still had a conservationist streak in me as regards
my own waterways, which, more than any of the wild rivers

of the world, have a right to be clean, that is, not spiked with toxic chemicals, not "doctored" or "altered" or "fixed". There are some things in this universe that are sacred. *Me*, for instance. And who agreed with me? Nobody agreed with me. Nobody but the Church.

If every man and every woman—fully human, fully alive, and complete in every detail—is made in the image and likeness of God, then we've got to protect and reverence what is natural and healthy. That is therapy: restoring the natural.

Pope Paul VI asserted (actually re-asserted) that the human design is not arbitrary, but providential. In particular, our sexual design (with its pleasurability and its fertility and its bond-ability) is not sick. We don't need to be "cured" of it. Our sexual powers are OK. They don't need to be "fixed".

If the Roman Pontiff had been a politician, he would have OK'd contraception. Virtually every social, political, scientific, and religious institution on earth was for it. Any politician can tell which way the wind is blowing; and any religious charlatan can get the drift and call it the Holy Spirit. But the Holy Spirit isn't just anything that's blowing in the wind. And Paul VI was not a politician.

In the face of incomprehension, scorn, and outright opposition on the part of—let's face it—nearly everybody, the Pope held up before our eyes the inviolability of the human design. You can reorganize the government and restructure the university; you can retool the economy and redesign society. But human beings as such—in our minds, our souls, our bodies, ourselves—are not to be redesigned. And this I hold to be decisive for the history of the human race. We must either perfect our wholeness, or repudiate it. If we repudiate it, there is little to prevent us from erasing ourselves finally, function by function, line by line. But if we perfect our wholeness, we will hold up before the eyes of the world the image of God.

KATERI TEKAKWITHA

Poetic names are ascribed to Kateri Tekakwitha—"Lily of the Mohawks", "Lily of New France", "Sainted Savage", "New America's New Star". All of them suggest beauty, originality or strength. Interesting tokens for a little orphan girl with semi-blind eyes, a pockmarked face, and the reputation among her own for being strange and lazy. "Tekakwitha", the more prosaic name given to the girl as a papoose, means "putting things in order". This was probably meant to be a good omen for daughterly luck with hearth and harvest. However, much to the rage of her coarse, warrior-like uncle, what Tekakwitha turned out to be able to put in order best was her spiritual house.

Her story begins in 1656 in the middle of a rich, virgin forest that seemed to stretch forever. Today the area is a thriving part of upstate New York. In the mid-seventeenth century it was the beautiful village Ossernenon—"the castle of the Turtles" —on the south bank of the Mohawk River. The natural landscape of the region was breathtakingly serene. But the character of the Mohawk tribe of the Iroquois who lived there could rise to savage cruelty.

Tekakwitha was the fruit of an unlikely marriage between a war chief and a gentle Christian. Kenhoronkwa, her father, had a thirst for conquest. Kahenta, her mother, had a thirst for God. They came together as captor and captive when Kenhoronkwa conquered the peace-loving Algonquin tribe, and the chief insisted on having her as his wife. Kahenta's sadness was softened by the knowledge that she was rescued from a captive's brutal labor. But the light of her life—the Christian God she had discovered through a sheltering French family and the holy Jesuit Black Robes—was shrouded in the

---

Kateri Tekakwitha is an example of a very courageous single woman and Native American saint.

center of her heart. If Chief Kenhoronkwa heard one word about the French or the Black Robes he shook with rage.

Kahenta took refuge in one secure Christian friendship with a middle-aged woman named Anastasia. They prayed silently side by side and were tender support to each other in the cruel, pagan atmosphere of their captors. Sometimes they would whisper when they were alone, speaking of God. The caution around these conversations might be compared with the agonies people go through while smuggling Bibles into a hostile land. One suspicion and someone pays.

I am sure Kahenta prayed silently that Tekakwitha and her infant son would one day be baptized. It is said that virtue passes easily from the hearts of mothers into the hearts of children. And young as she was, Tekakwitha carried much of Kahenta in her soul. She never outgrew her gentleness or sweet nature and when she later found God she felt as though she had always known him.

When she was only four, Tekakwitha lost her mother. She also lost her father and brother, alone surviving a frightening sweep of smallpox across the tribe. Not understanding the disease, the Mohawks were frenzied. At night, greased with colored paint, the warriors danced and whooped around a campfire, offering victims to Manitou, the spirit of evil, and Aireskoi, the demon of war. Medicine men pulled up herbs in the moonlight and sorcerers chanted. The people perceived the smallpox as a mysterious spell—a punishment for not conquering enough tribes.

After Chief Kenhoronkwa and Kahenta and their young son died, Anastasia took Tekakwitha under her wing. Presumably the child was wrapped in layers of doeskin, and rocked near the fire. It seems a miracle that she survived, but she was meant to survive. She had an important part to play for her people.

Lifelong scars seemed to be the price that Tekakwitha paid for surviving such a harsh disease. Her eyes were never the same; at first she cupped her hands over them at the slightest crack of light. Her legs were weakened; she had to learn to walk again. And her beautiful young cheeks were pitted, forever marring her loveliness. This latter suffering turned out to be a special cross among the Mohawk women who were very vain and conscious of looks. It isolated Tekakwitha. At the same time it made her tender and made her later discovery of God eager and ecstatic. At last she found One who could see past her scars and love her for her very self.

Tekakwitha's new guardians were the new chief Iowerano (her father's brother), his wife Karitha, and his sister Arosen. They didn't have particular affection for their frail niece, but she posed fresh advantages for their greed. Iowerano had no children of his own, and Tekakwitha could be a doting housemaid. Also, much more to the point, Mohawk maidens were the lifeblood of the tribe. They learned useful arts like sewing, cooking, and harvesting. And they lured a young brave into the family, an extra hunter, who would enrich the household with furs and game. Among the Iroquois Mohawks, a young man marrying a girl would enter her family home and be a point of pride and source of goods.

This plan was all very practical for the clever uncle and his clan. But Tekakwitha would have nothing to do with it. Even before she was baptized, Tekakwitha shrank from marriage. To grasp this anomaly fully, we must look at the Mohawk culture of her day. First, it was heavily matriarchal. The women ruled; they chose their men; they harvested the nourishment, advised the tribe, and begot new life. Marriage was almost a fixture of power for Mohawk women; virginity was a disgrace.

But Tekakwitha was true to some inner call to stay apart. Later this love of solitude would blossom into a love union with God. In the meantime, it kept the distasteful culture of the Mohawks at arms' length. Once she married into it, she would entwine herself in a hundred other rituals she hated: scalpings, wild feasts and dances, sacrificing captives to appease false gods, and eating the victims' flesh.

Chief Iowerano's wife and sister were persistent, though.

They tricked Tekakwitha in little ways, teasing her about various braves in the tribe. Once, after Karitha brushed her hair and braided it with colored beads, she told her how nice it would be to take a refreshing bowl of corn meal to Blue Fox when he arrived home after the hunt. Always loving to be kind, Tekakwitha agreed. Just in time, she caught on to the game and ran from the long bark house. When a Mohawk maiden wished to marry a man, she went up to him and offered corn meal. It was a simple gesture, but sealed a marriage. Incidents like that put Tekakwitha on guard in her own home.

But joy came quietly into Tekakwitha's life when a treaty was passed, finally, between the French and all the Iroquois tribes. The Mohawks never would have chosen such a humiliating alliance, but circumstances forced them to in 1667. From that point on, the French Jesuit Black Robes had a right to come into the Mohawk village, to sleep and eat among the Indians, and to preach about "Rawenniio", the true God.

Tekakwitha was forbidden to speak to the Black Robes. Her uncle and aunts kept a constant vigilance on the girl, almost as though they were jealous of her deeper love for something they couldn't see or touch: the God of her mother, the God that was enchanting others in their tribe, a God whose ways were gentle and forgiving rather than warlike.

One day Father James de Lamberville, a newcomer to the Mohawk village, walked past the Chief's house, hurrying past the door because he knew it was the one place he was forbidden to enter. A moment later, though, a very strong impulse drew him back. He found himself approaching the doorway and looking in. Tekakwitha—on a rare day that she was not working in the maize fields—was alone inside. At the sight of the Black Robe, Tekakwitha poured out her longings to be baptized and take instruction. She told Father de Lamberville about Kahenta, her Christian mother, and about all her pent up desires in her pagan home.

The French priest did teach Tekakwitha about God the Father, God the Son, and the Great Holy Spirit. He taught her about the sacraments and the saints, how to pray the rosary, and how to lift her heart to God all during the day. The transformation of Tekakwitha from a cheerful, gracious girl to a joyous, glowing one was evident to all. And on Easter Sunday, 1676, she received the waters of baptism.

In a fairy tale, this might be a happy ending. But the characters who had always given Tekakwitha a rough time did not melt away into the background. They got madder and they got meaner.

When Tekakwitha kept holy the Lord's Day, on Sunday, the women hissed at her and told her she was lazy. Little children threw rocks at her and laughed at her. Chief Iowerano regarded her as stupid and a disgrace. Amid all this, Tekakwitha continued to respect and wait on her family, hand and foot. Her humility and cheerfulness only made them taunt her more, even going so far as to withhold her meals and leave her outside when it was cold. But the only issue Tekakwitha— now *Kateri*, or Catherine, Tekakwitha since her baptismal day—really cared about was keeping intact her precious religious freedom, and that had blessedly become her matter of choice.

Watching all this, Father de Lamberville asked Kateri Tekakwitha if she would be willing to make the secret journey to Canada to live among other Christians. At first, Kateri was afraid; the Mohawk village was many terrible things, but it was her home. She knew all its woods and streams like the back of her hand. Those woods had become her Cathedral in prayerful moments, and she loved them.

But slowly the seed of hope that the priest had dropped into her heart grew into a desire that no one could deny.

Late one night, while her uncle and aunts slept and the whole village was quiet, Kateri Tekakwitha heard the sound of an owl. It was a noise made by her guide. She cautiously ran from her house and met Hot Ashes at a special tree in the forest. Moments later, one of the aunts awoke, saw her missing, and roused the whole village. Chief Iowerano gave orders to his men to shoot to kill.

Kateri was worried about endangering the life of Hot Ashes. When she whispered this to him, he gave her a stone. He told her that when the men were close upon her, she was to throw the stone in his direction—away from where she hid. Hot Ashes, knowing the forest well, was able to get away, and through his advice to Kateri, God spared her life. Later they were reunited, and he guided her through the miles of quiet forest. Then they took his canoe up the western shore of Lake George toward the south bank of the St. Lawrence—rowing upstream between the crimson leaves of Canadian maples. It was autumn, 1677.

On the shores, welcoming Kateri Tekakwitha "home" were the missionary priests and her mother's dearest friend Anastasia. Kateri handed a note to the missionary priests that had been handwritten by the Black Robe who taught her and brought her into the Faith. It simply said, "I send you Kateri Tekakwitha, a treasure. Guard her well."

Kateri Tekakwitha only lived a few short years after that, for she died at age twenty-three. But the rest of her life was spent all for God, loving him and loving everyone around her. She was tireless in helping the aged and sick, and she taught young children. All four seasons of the year she arose at four o'clock in the morning to walk to church. Often she did this barefoot in the snow. She heard two Masses every day, joined the Sodality of Mary, and frequently visited our Lord in the Most Blessed Sacrament.

Kateri Tekakwitha was a person that few could figure out. She was terribly pockmarked and frail, and yet when they looked at her she radiated an irresistible loveliness. The Christian Indians that knew her in Canada loved to watch her and be near her, because she was almost like a breath of heaven.

She was different, and she brought a very rare beauty into their lives.

Kateri Tekakwitha reminds me very much of the main character in a beautiful allegory by Hannah Hurnard called *Hinds' Feet on High Places*. Much Afraid, a girl with a slightly crippled walk and a crooked mouth, *longs* to go with the Shepherd to the High Places. Her relatives try to intimidate and bully her, and logic suggests that she might give in. But a seed of love is in her heart, and she follows him anyway, making her ascent hand in hand with Sorrow and Suffering. Like Much Afraid, Kateri Tekakwitha did make it to the top, to the High Places. And in so doing, she lived up to God's blueprint of her lovely self which he had dreamed of for all eternity.

On Being a
Consecrated Woman

Some of my closest friends are religious women consecrated to the Lord. In knowing them and in reading the lives of vowed saints, I have come to appreciate the beauty of the choice of being a bride of Christ. We all can be brides of Christ, spiritually; but the consecrated woman dedicates her whole life to him without the mediation of any creatures.

Two groups of nuns that I know best are Benedictines. I feel close to two communities which are very different in externals. The sisters at Pecos monastery are outwardly very contemporary with casual dress, some with long, long hair. The nuns at St. Scholastica's are traditionally garbed and appear to be more recollected.

When I visit these groups, I see that their lives are not unlike mine. They have time in the "family" at meals, they have a time of formal praise of the Liturgy of the Hours and daily Mass, time for the Spouse alone, time to be motherly in making meals, cleaning, talking to guests. They radiate quiet joy.

They look much more fulfilled in a *womanly* way than many a wife and mother, and this seems to be a proof of their spiritual femininity.

Sister Mary Ann Follmar writes beautifully about the joys of consecration:

THE CONSECRATED VIRGIN:
AN ICON OF THE CHURCH

The consecration of virgins is an ancient rite in the life of the Church which, since 1970, has become more widely known and bestowed. What does it mean to be a consecrated virgin? For me, it means that through the intense fire of Jesus' love I became, as it were, an icon of the Church through receiving the consecration of a virgin. As a result, I am called to imitate the Virgin Mary as virgin, bride, and mother.

To be a virgin consecrated to the Lord implies not only physical virginity but also virginity of mind and heart. In other words, my whole being is to be focused on Jesus. In order that this will happen to an ever greater degree, it is imperative that I engage in much prayer and in discipline of affections, time, thought, and words. Each day I must give myself anew to the Lord and place my entire being before him in love.

But I am also a bride since I have been solemnly espoused to Jesus Christ. Hence, I need to be a radiant love sign in the life of the Church, a sign whereby other persons can see the beauty of being wholly captivated by God. In my own life, I realized in joyful astonishment one day that I was very much in love with the Lord who had chosen me to be his spouse and that this relationship was the source of immense happiness in my life. This friendship compels me to spend much time in the Eucharistic Presence in order to rejoice in the Lord's love and to grow in that love. The spousal relationship also causes me to take into my heart the concerns of the Lord Jesus, especially the division and rebellion in his Church as well as the pain caused by atheism and materialism. Awareness of these problems coupled with certitude of God's mercy has caused me to become an intercessor for the Church and the world.

Finally, I am also a mother in the spiritual order since love is always life-giving. It is my great privilege to nurture the life of Jesus in people by preparing them to share more intensely in the sacraments, by forming them in the ecclesial spirit, and by directing them in prayer. This way of motherhood is a precious gift. In fact, by being the spouse of the Lord and exercising a spiritual motherhood, I feel completely fulfilled as a woman.

The theme of being a bride of Christ and of the Holy Spirit makes Mary a beautiful patroness for consecrated women. This relationship was part of the spirituality of Saint Maximilian Kolbe, founder of the Immaculata movement.[1] Phyllis Schabow, a Marian Woman in Ministry, writes about this spirituality:

> Back in the 1940s, a wonderful man by the name of Maximilian Kolbe, a Franciscan priest publishing a magazine called *Immaculata*, sketched out an idea without going into it fully. He didn't have time; he had to go to Auschwitz and die a martyr. But soon after Vatican II a Dominican priest living in Rome came across Kolbe's statements, immediately set aside his own work on our Lady, and began delving into the works of Maximilian. A beautiful book emerged called *Immaculate Conception and the Holy Spirit*. In it the Dominican saw that Kolbe had

---

[1] The Immaculata movement, or *Militia Immaculata*, is an international Marian movement based on Total Consecration to our Lady and the spirituality of Maximilian Kolbe. The movement is concerned with the spiritual formation of its members and world-wide Catholic evangelization.

discovered the essential union of the Blessed Virgin Mary with her Spouse, the Holy Spirit, who was himself the Immaculate Conception of the love of the Eternal Father for the Adorable Son. He, the Holy Spirit, being himself *Immaculate Conception* could rightly transfer his own name to his spouse, and indeed, he did. At the instant of the conception of the adorable human body of the Woman of Genesis who had been in the mind and Heart of God from all eternity—his own very special love, she who was to become the Mother of the God/Man, and the Mother of all the elect, was given that privilege that was proper to God alone—the name and the fact of *Immaculate Conception*. She was not just created in a state of whiteness with regard to her soul, but she was to be *Whiteness* itself. She was to encompass a Man who is God from all eternity, and God dwells in *Light Inaccessible*—which is our Lady.

TERESA OF AVILA

For many reasons Teresa of Avila (1515–1562) radiates as one of the most profoundly beautiful women of human history. On the one hand she was blessed with the genius and leadership to found and govern the Discalced Carmelite monasteries, write brilliant spiritual works, and become the first woman Doctor of the Church. On the other hand, she was very human, exuding all the natural graces that make a person most lovable. She was outgoing, affectionate, vivacious, charming, and witty. She was passionate, articulate, and beautiful. Because of these rich, magnetic pulls within her personality, Teresa of Jesus spent a good twenty years of her convent life torn

The words of Saint Teresa quoted in this story can be found in *The Life of St. Teresa of Avila* (Newman Press, 1962) and *Interior Castle* (Image Books, 1961).

between the joys of contemplative prayer and the more human delights of conversation in the parlor.

In the Prologue of her autobiography, she tells us up front:

> Among the saints who were converted to God, I have never found one in whom I have any comfort. For I see that they, after our Lord had called them, never fell into sin again; I not only became worse, but, as it seems to me, deliberately withstood the graces of His Majesty, because I saw that I was thereby bound to serve him more earnestly, knowing at the same time that I could not pay the least portion of my debt.
>
> May he be blessed forever who waited for me so long!

In the autobiographical chapters following this disclosure, the Spanish mystic, looking back on her life, remembers the peaks and valleys of her soul on its journey. The beginnings of the journey were rocky.

As a little girl, she was spirited and hard to pin down. At seven years of age, for example, she schemed with her favorite brother Rodrigo to run away from home to be beheaded by the Moors.

> When I read of the martyrdom undergone by the saints for the love of God, it struck me that the vision of God was very cheaply purchased; and I had a great desire to die a martyr's death—not out of any love for him of which I was conscious, but that I might most quickly attain to those great joys of heaven.

As they crossed the bridge out of town, an uncle spotted the children and returned them to their mother who had been combing Avila for them frantically.

In adolescence, Teresa candidly portrays herself as vain, wilful, and easily swayed by a worldly, gossipy girl cousin.

This friendship distressed my father and sister exceedingly. They often blamed me for it; but, as they could not hinder that person from coming into the house, all their efforts were in vain; for I was very adroit in doing anything that was wrong.

Exasperating behavior aside, Teresa writes that of the twelve children in her family "I was the most cherished by my father." She was the person he loved most in the world. Perhaps that is why he took pains, after the death of her mother and the marriage of her sister, to place her in a convent boarding school, the Augustinian monastery of Our Lady of Grace. This move was intended to protect Teresa from her worldly companions, although outside friends still found ways to communicate with her, smuggling letters and presents into the convent walls. One young suitor in particular spoke of marriage.

At this point in her life, Teresa did not want to be a nun, although she was afraid of marriage. "I had a great dislike to being a nun . . . and this had become deeply ingrained in me." The conflict inside her to make a choice was so pronounced and constant that she fell gravely ill and had to return home to her father's house. Teresa did not realize it, but this would occasion an important turning point in her life.

On a journey out into the country, Teresa and her father stopped to visit her uncle, Don Pedro de Cepeda, a devout widower who was contemplating a religious life. This kindly old man had a library full of books and persuaded his eighteen-year-old niece to read them to him. Although bored by the prospect, Teresa politely agreed and was astonished to discover a slow awakening of new resolve in herself:

The impression made on my heart by the words of God, both as read and heard, and the excellence of my uncle's company made me understood that all things are nothing, and that the world is vanity and will soon pass away. I began to fear that, if I had died of my illness, I should have gone to hell.

Reading the letters of Saint Jerome and other spiritual classics it dawned on Teresa that the only way to save her soul was behind a convent wall.

> I could not incline my will to being a nun, but saw it was the best and safest state, and so, little by little, I determined to force myself to embrace it. . . . The decision to enter the religious life seems to have been inspired by servile fear more than by love.

Despite the lack of ecstatic enthusiasm, Teresa resolved that she would make a life for herself at the Convent of the Incarnation in Avila. The one obstacle was her father, who expressed grief and denial. Characteristically wilful, Teresa ran away from home, even as her passionate heart was breaking. She vividly shares this heartache in her autobiography:

> I remember—and I really believe this is true—that when I left my father's house my distress was so great that I do not think it will be greater when I die. It seemed to me as if every bone in my body were being wrenched asunder for as I had no love of God, to subdue my love for my father and kinsfolk, everything was such a strain to me that, if the Lord had not helped me, no reflection of my own would have sufficed to keep me true to my purpose. But the Lord gave me courage to fight against myself and so I carried out my intention.

For the remainder of her life, Teresa would look back and praise God for inspiring her to act on her reluctant decision. Favors, joys, tenderness, and delight blessed her novitiate year.

> When I was spending time in sweeping floors which I had previously spent on my own indulgence and adornment,

I realized that I was now free from all those things and there came to me a new joy.

For the first twenty years of religious life, Teresa lived as a very ordinary nun. She writes of the distractions which kept her from prayer and urges strict enclosure for contemplative nuns. After this period of time, she had an inward conversion of more perfect surrender to God.

Courage, she told her sisters, is needed in prayer, the courage to begin and to persevere. She, of all people, knew the turmoil of desiring to keep a foot in both worlds, the world of silence and the world of sense. She writes about Christians torn between Christ and the world in her reference to "the Second Mansion":

> They gradually get nearer to the place where his Majesty dwells. He becomes a very good neighbor to them. Such are his mercy and goodness that, even when we are engaged in our worldly pastimes and business and pleasure and keep falling into sins and rising again . . . he calls us ceaselessly, time after time, to approach him.

Teresa discovered, thanks to a saintly Franciscan introduced to her by her uncle Don Pedro, the powers of mental prayer and contemplation. Christ, she writes, quickly granted her the favor of leading her into the Prayer of Quiet and occasionally even to Union.

Gradually, visions, ecstasies, locutions, and the highest realms of mystical prayer became frequent realities in Teresa's life. Teresa always considered herself far beneath these sweet overtures from Christ, and yet she courageously made all of them bear fruit. She followed God's call to restore and edify the corrupted Carmel she had entered. With John of the Cross she braved tedious and unnerving obstacles in raising up sixteen other monasteries loyal to the original Carmelite Rule. She directed and inspired holiness in the lives of many women and achieved high sanctity in her own. She brought into the

Church a new spirit of harmony, order, and love. And though Teresa was uneducated, with no trace of intellectual or theological training, she wrote masterpieces on mystical prayer and spiritual truth.

It cannot be overestimated that Teresa's core of strength came from Jesus himself. To her, Christ was more directly present as a known and loved person than any of those with whom she was in daily contact. Love of Jesus was the essence of her spiritual life. The themes of deep and intimate love for him and constant union with him in prayer recur over and over in her books.

Even though her own unusual life teemed with visions and mystical favors, she goes on to explain in her practical and down-to-earth insights:

> His appeals come through the conversations of good people, from sermons, good books . . . or they come through sicknesses and trials, or means of truths which God teaches us at times when we are engaged in prayer.

Teresa's refreshing approach to God as a friend, lover, and confidant makes her a saint with enormous appeal.

One nobleman from Avila who supported the sisters called her "the world's magnet". He said about her:

> [I could spend] All day long with her without noticing the time, and all night long in the hope of seeing her again next day, for her way of speaking was delightful—and the word *gracioso* in Spanish adds a touch of wit to the delightfulness and her conversation was pleasant and at the same time serious, simple, and full of good sense. She was so much on fire with the love of God. The warmth radiating from her words was so gently persuasive that it melted the hearts of all who came in contact with her without causing them pain; for among her qualities she possessed *gratia sermonis*, graciousness of speech, and drew to her, as she wanted them and for whatever purpose she wanted them,

all who heard her. It might have been said that she held in her hand the helm that steers all hearts.

Harmless fun was admitted by Teresa to be in harmony with holiness. "What would become of our little house", she addressed her nuns, "if each of you hid the little wit you possess!" On another occasion she bluntly told them, "From silly devotions and from sour-faced saints, good Lord deliver us!" In her older years, when she fell in the mud while traveling on a mission for her Lord, she asked God, "Why should I who am doing Thy work be so badly treated?" "Thus do I treat my friends", God answered. "No wonder, then," said Teresa, "that you have so few."

The same God once appeared to Teresa and asked her name. "I am Teresa of Jesus", she told him, to which he replied, "I am Jesus of Teresa."

Teresa of Jesus shows the heights to which all of us can ascend. She shows us the way and teaches us that our deepest and most satisfying joys, our treasures and all our hope, is in our Lord Jesus Christ. Most of us, like Teresa, travel a long road before we can reach the point of perfect and holy integrity of heart. But with prayer, grace, and the infinite love of God, all is possible.

Saint Teresa's Bookmark

> Let nothing disturb thee;
> Nothing afright thee;
> All things are passing:
> God never changes.
> Patience attains
> All that it strives for
> He who has God
> Finds he lacks nothing
> God alone suffices.

Enjoying Our
Feminine Traits

Love of Beauty

The perfect decks itself in beauty out of love for the imperfect.

Tagore

By means of the created beauty around us, Christ knocks at the door of our soul telling us that we should love him who is the author and creator of this beauty.

Rich

For Christ plays in ten thousand places, lovely in limbs,
  and lovely in eyes not his
To the Father through the features of men's faces.

Hopkins

I love these quotations by men about beauty. More often, however, do I find women seeking to discover beauty in the everyday:

Inebriate of air am I
And debauchee of dew,
Reeling, through endless summer days,
From inns of molten blue.

Emily Dickinson

The pure taste of the apple is as much a contact with the beauty of the universe as the contemplation of a picture by Cezanne. And more people are capable of savouring apple sauce than of contemplating Cezanne.

Simone Weil

I think because of our long tradition as house decorators and gardeners many women have had a greater opportunity than most men to develop love of beauty in a homey way.

Also, because women tend to be able to express their emotions more freely, we are more inclined to luxuriate in the gift of beauty, sending up to God songs of praise for the loveliness of nature, of faces, of music and art.

I especially love finding unlikely beauty. I think of it as a surprise from God who is waiting for me to catch on and be delighted. Oftentimes the cause of ignoring God's gift is my temperamental melancholy, so that my spare thoughts are so caught up in brooding worry that I miss the flowers.

My great mentor, Dietrich von Hildebrand, was a vocal lover of beauty. He could not pass anything beautiful without remarking on it. Responding to the value intrinsic in everything around us is a good antidote to the tense grimness that afflicts many of us, especially if we are sensitive to the many evils around us.

I cannot think about beauty without remembering the Canticle of Saint Francis of Assisi. I will include it here and suggest that after reading it you might make up a canticle of your own.

The Canticle of the Sun

O most high, almighty, good Lord God, to you belong
  praise, glory, honor, and all blessing!
Praised be my Lord God with all his creatures; and
  especially our brother the sun, who brings us the day,
  and who brings us the light; fair is he, and shining with
  a very great splendor: O Lord, to us he signifies you!
Praised be my Lord for our sister the moon, and for the
  stars, which he has set clear and lovely in heaven.
Praised be my Lord for our brother the wind, and for air
  and cloud, calms and all weather, by which you uphold
  in life all creatures.
Praised be my Lord for our sister water, who is very
  serviceable to us, and humble, and precious and clean.
Praised be my Lord for our brother fire, through whom
  you give us light in the darkness; and he is bright, and
  pleasant, and very mighty and strong.
Praised be my Lord for our mother the earth, which
  sustains us and keeps us, and brings forth divers fruits,
  and flowers of many colors, and grass.

And here are some lovely poems about beauty by Marian
Women:

On a chase
a race with the wind
spiraling upward toward
the sky in a golden swirl.
Red leaves, yellow leaves,
burnished by the sun
and I the runner in
wild pursuit
to grasp a thing of beauty
in my hand
for just a moment.

Melinda Brogan

The Roses of Beatitudes

One special day eons ago,
  God looked with love
    Upon His creation;
Under his gaze
  A flower grew,
    Unfolding its arms—
    Love's gaze to embrace.
The first rose bloomed
  As love filled its face.

Roses,
Trimmed, picked and arranged
Into lovely bouquets;
  Soft and bold colors
    Blending
Our pleasure to behold
  Upon God's altars
Fragrance scent,
  Like prayers ascending . . .

Until
Heads bowed low,
  Petals fading, roses dying—
    Sweet odor of sanctity
    The fullness of love given . . .

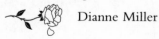

Dianne Miller

Sweetness

In my book *Feminine, Free, and Faithful*,[1] I spend some time analyzing feminine traits. The quality of sweetness, seemingly to be identified with the feminine more than with the masculine (even though we all know lots of awfully sweet men) is widely misunderstood. Many women have come to dislike even the word "sweet". It can call up the idea of a woman who is sugary, gushing, sentimental, mawkish. I myself used to think of sweetness in that way, contrasting it with strength and individuality. The best way to understand real sweetness, however, is to consider its opposite: bitterness. How many women do you know who pride themselves on being bitter! Bitterness usually springs from unwillingness to forgive. Long-held resentment makes a woman quick on the draw when it comes to sarcasm, expressed or interior (for, of course, we all know what it is like to put on a sweet face while inwardly grinding our teeth).

Sweetness is also an opposite to a sort of closed withdrawn quality that we have when we are too much involved with our own poor selves to be responsively open to others in their needs, their hurts. A woman, or man, who is called sweet, is usually a person of sensitive perceptiveness, whose heart easily vibrates to the feelings of others. Some time ago I gave some workshop-retreats to the nuns and monks of Pecos Benedictine monastery. There were certainly ten or more women of an incomparable sweetness and their presence was such a soothing joy to all. These same women seemed always concerned

[1] *Feminine, Free, and Faithful* is also published by Ignatius Press, San Francisco.

about the feelings of others. The women in my parish
Spirit of Mary group are also resplendent in sweetness.

Genuine sweetness, as opposed to manipulative pseudo-
sweetness, is also an opposite to bossiness. The sweet
woman wants to serve rather than to dominate. I find
that as soon as I want to seize control of a situation, my
sweetness disappears and a certain strained zeal comes to
the fore, leading others to back away as fast as they can.

You may notice that sweetness most usually goes
along with humor. Why? Because life does seem very
humorous when we let go enough to see that Jesus saves
and that he must look at lots of situations with amuse-
ment. If I am trying to redeem the world myself, then I'd
better be dead serious about it, since the job is infinitely
beyond my capacities.

Sweetness also has a lot to do with obedience, another
highly disprized virtue in our times, especially for women.
Obedience to legitimate authority takes one out of the
driver's seat into a position of making the "ride" more
enjoyable by being pleasant and affable.

As a spiritual exercise, perhaps for Lent, we might
watch ourselves and see when sweetness departs. Is it
because I am harboring resentment? Am I being over-
controlling? Do I want to usurp the authority of others in
order to put through schemes which may simply not be
God's will, at least not for this moment?

Diane Prucher, a Marian Woman, writes that "spiritual
sweetness ultimately rests with God's gifts and graces. . . .
Perhaps our lives are stepping stones to the ultimate
sweetness of light and love resting just ahead on the

paths of contemplation and resurrection. My personal life has been a testimony that strength and intelligence dressed in sweetness deal best with ungodly people and their problems."

THÉRÈSE OF LISIEUX

In the spring of 1858, a man and a woman crossed paths on a bridge in France.

The man, Louis Martin, was heartsick because he longed to cloister himself as an Augustinian monk in the monastery of the Great Saint Bernard, high in the Alps, but he had been rejected for his lack of classical education.

The woman, Zélie Guerin, was crestfallen because her life-long dream of becoming a nun had been dashed by a mother superior who denied her entrance to the convent and pointed her back in the direction of the world.

As so often is the case, God allowed these puzzling obstacles to happiness; and in so doing, he ensured that Louis Martin and Zélie Guerin would both be available that spring of 1858 to embark together on a life of spiritual glory that far surpassed their original hopes. For three months after their footsteps crossed on the bridge, Louis and Zélie were married one midnight at the church of Notre Dame in Alençon, France. In time they would have nine children, and the ninth—known all over the world today as 'The Little Flower'—turned out to be one of the greatest saints of modern times.

This special little girl was born to the world late on the night of January 2, 1872, and a few days later was baptized Marie-

Many of the quotes of Saint Thérèse used in this story can be found in her autobiography, *Story of a Soul* (ICS, 1975). Others are from the memoirs of her sister Céline and other sources (see bibliography).

François-Thérèse. Interestingly, it is recorded that shortly after the child's birth a young man whom Mr. Martin had rescued from destitution knocked at the door of the Martin home and handed the family a heartfelt self-composed verse: "Surrounded as you are with loving care and tender love, smile at the dawn of life and grow quickly for, though now only a tiny bud, you will one day be a rose." A century later, we smile in wonder at the young writer's prophetic choice of words.

From the beginning, Thérèse was cherished like a princess. A month before her birth, Madame Zélie confided to her brother how passionately she loved babies and that she believed she had been born solely to have children; at age forty-one, and battling breast cancer, she feared this child would be her last. Moreover, four of her eight beloved children had already died in infancy and young childhood.

This ninth child—a fifth living daughter—was so treasured that when Zélie saw she was a weak and sickly baby, she beseeched a robust farmer's wife, a nursemaid named Rose Taille, to take Thérèse into her country home and fields to nurse and nourish her. Much to Mr. Taille's consternation, his busy peasant spouse welcomed the little one under her wing for fifteen months, probably saving the saint's life. That summer Zélie wrote of Thérèse: "Her nurse brings her out to the fields in a wheelbarrow, seated on top of a load of hay; she hardly ever cries. Rose says that one could hardly find a better child." Once healthy and home again, the blond, blue-eyed, impish toddler quickly became the family favorite. In time Thérèse's father would call her his "little queen".

A current of love and merriment runs through all the portrayals of early life in the Martin home. It was a colorful household filled with the Victorian charms of Zélie's exquisite lacemaking, Louis' kindly, artistic ways, and the lively, delightful presence of five very feminine little girls.

In August 1877, however, when Thérèse was four years old, a shadow passed over all of their lives. Zélie Martin, at age forty-five, died, leaving an inconsolable husband and five vulnerable young daughters. At this turning point the Martins did something which they never would have done had Zélie survived; they uprooted from their comfortable Alençon home to move close to an aunt, uncle, and cousins in Lisieux. It was a decisive move, for it also landed the Martin family within walking distance of the Carmelite gardens and cloister of Lisieux. Four of the five Martin daughters would slip through those walls.

Happily for us, the tight-knit bond forged between the girls after their mother's death kept them together—for if it were not for the requests of Thérèse's own sisters at Carmel that she record her memories as a "family souvenir", she would never have been known to us today. Her potent secrets of holiness would have remained as enshrouded as the cloister.

From the tender ages of five to fifteen, Thérèse lived in a house in Lisieux called Les Buissonnets. Despite the absence of gas, electricity, and running water—typical of French country houses a century ago—Les Buissonnets with its lush garden, and its menagerie of hens and rabbits, proved a golden haven for the Martins. An imaginative child, Thérèse often filled her miniature tea service with seeds and leaves and bits of bark, then solemnly carried it across the lawn to her father who, in turn, pretended to savor the brew. Thérèse later remembered these years as being "enveloped in love", and the foundation of her childlike approach to God in later life.

This love was too rich to stay just within the Martin circle. Every Monday morning a gathering of the poor and homeless would arrive at the doorstep of Les Buissonnets for money and food. These, and stray beggars who turned up on other days of the week, were never turned away empty-handed. Moreover, Monsieur Martin never left the house without his pockets full, just in case he encountered a person in need. His constant kindness to the less fortunate made Les Buissonnets a school of charity for his children.

It was also from Les Buissonnets that little Thérèse and her father, hand in hand, would go out walking every afternoon. "We made our visit to the Blessed Sacrament together, going to a different church each day, and it was in this way we entered the Carmelite chapel for the first time. Papa showed me the choir grille and told me there were nuns behind it. I was far from thinking at the time that nine years later I would be in their midst!"

The blond ringlets and lace collars in Thérèse's early photographs frame the face of an angel; but growing up, Thérèse was not without her faults. As a small, pampered child she was wilful and given to tantrums. Later, as a young schoolgirl Thérèse was inclined to be melancholy, dreading Sunday nights as the prelude to school the next morning. Shy and ultra-sensitive, she recoiled from the usual schoolgirl gossip and games.

At home, too, she was super-sensitive and her strong emotions had a short fuse. She writes: "I was really unbearable because of my extreme touchiness; if, without meaning to, I slightly upset someone I loved, I burst into a flood of tears instead of mastering myself, and that, of course, made matters worse. And when I began to cheer up I wept again for having wept. All arguments were useless; I was quite unable to correct this terrible fault."

All of this was changed, however, on the night of Christmas, 1886, when Thérèse experienced a grace-filled conversion from the Christ Child. "I felt *charity* enter into my soul, and the need to forget myself and to please others." Years later she would write that this Christmas night was the dividing point in her life, a night after which her introspective, melancholic sensitivity was transformed into a virtuous sensitivity full of courage and beauty. She was thirteen years old.

Slowly a fire began burning in Thérèse; it was a fire of love, a love for God and a love for souls. A striking account in her autobiography focuses on Henri Pranzini, an Italian criminal who had stolen the jewels of a woman in Paris, then murdered the woman together with her child and maid—a theft and triple-murder crowning a lifetime of evil deeds. Finally caught and condemned to death, Pranzini only boasted of his crimes to the executioners and mocked religion.

"Everything pointed to the fact that he would die impenitent", Thérèse later wrote, "I wanted at all costs to prevent him from falling into hell, and to attain my purpose I employed every means imaginable. Feeling that by myself I could do nothing, I offered to God all the infinite merits of our Lord. . . ."

Pranzini remained blasphemous and defiant up until the end. But on August 31, 1887, the day of his execution, as he mounted the scaffold of the guillotine and was preparing to place his head beneath the blade, he suddenly turned, took hold of the crucifix the priest held out to him, and kissed the sacred wounds three times. "Then," wrote Thérèse in triumph, "his soul went to receive the merciful sentence of him who declares in heaven there will be more joy over one sinner who repents than over ninety-nine just who have no need to repent!"

At fourteen, Thérèse's vibrant attraction to God and her desire to save souls made the Carmelite cloister an enticing challenge. Two of her sisters, Pauline and Marie, were within the cloister already. Thérèse's difficulty was in approaching her father. When her sisters left home she had thought her own heart would break. She imagined that he, too, would suffer deeply in letting her go.

On the feast of Pentecost she finally got up her nerve. "He was seated by the well," she remembered, "and without saying a word, I sat down by his side, my eyes already wet with tears. He gazed at me tenderly, and taking my head he placed it on his heart, saying: 'What's the matter, my little Queen? Tell me.' Then rising as though to hide his own emotion, he walked while still holding my head on his heart."

Monsieur Martin listened to Thérèse quietly with his own tears; at last he nodded his consent. Then he walked her over to a low wall, pointed out some small white flowers, picked one, and gave it to her. He talked about the care with which God had brought it into being and preserved it to that very day. "As I listened," Thérèse recalled, "I believed I was hearing my own story, so great was the resemblance between what Jesus had done for the *little flower* and *little Thérèse*. I accepted it as a relic and noticed that, in gathering it, Papa had pulled all its *roots* out without breaking them. It seemed destined to live on in another soil more fertile than the tender moss where it had spent its first days."

Thérèse entered the "new soil" of Carmel on April 9, 1888, the day the community was celebrating the feast of the Annunciation. Fifteen years old, she had battled to be received into the cloister so young. One of the most touching portrayals in her autobiography is that of herself breaking the silence of a group of French pilgrims in Rome, rushing forward to ask the Pope, eye to eye, if he would bless her early entrance to Carmel; that day she had purposely twisted her long, thick hair up in a bun to appear older. The Pope seemed impressed, and in time, Mother Marie de Gonzague, the Prioress, consented, partly against better judgment.

But the new postulant quickly won her over. Mother Marie later raved of Thérèse in a personal letter: "Tall and robust, with a childlike face, and with a tone of voice and expression that hide a wisdom, a perfection, and a perspicacity of a woman of *fifty*. . . . A mystic, a *comedienne*, she is everything! She can make you shed tears of devotion, and she can as easily make you split your sides with laughter during recreation."

It was the desire to be a saint, and a *great* saint, though, that made Sister Thérèse forge the Little Way of Spiritual Childhood for which she is so well loved and known. *The Story of a Soul*, the saint's autobiography which illuminates this Little Way, created an international stir after her death and has today been translated into over forty languages, reaching millions.

Her Little Way was direct, uncomplicated, and accessible to everyone. From early childhood she had desired to become a saint, but whenever she read about the spiritual giants, their holiness reminded her of the peak of a towering mountain lost in the clouds. She knew she could never climb those rugged heights, yet she refused to believe that God would inspire her to an impossible goal. The thought came to her that in certain houses an elevator takes the place of stairs. She started to look for an "elevator" that would lift her, with all her imperfections, straight to God.

In her search, she discovered a line in Proverbs (9:4): "Whoever is a little one let him come to me." What would God do for the little one, she wondered. God answered her through the mouth of Isaiah (66:12): "I shall carry you at my breast and on my knee I shall caress you."

Asked what was meant by remaining a little child before God, Thérèse said, "It is to acknowledge that we possess nothing ourselves and that everything comes to us from God; to admit that we cannot accomplish anything of ourselves but expect everything from him . . . to make ourselves smaller and smaller, and more and more trusting and confident, so he will lift us up and *carry us in his arms*." Thérèse said she would adopt this way of total trust in God's mercy and love "even if I had on my conscience every imaginable crime".

In her way of spiritual childhood, Thérèse slashed the "red tape" that holds back countless souls from trying to be close to God. "There are great saints who have *won* heaven by their works," Thérèse said one day, "but my favorite patrons are those who *stole* it—like the Holy Innocents and the Good Thief. I want to imitate these thieves and win heaven by a stratagem, a stratagem of love which will open its gates to me and to all poor sinners with me." The way, she believed, was to love, to love deeply without counting the cost, and then abandon oneself with total trust and confidence to the good God.

She once illustrated her point using a story she had listened to in childhood: A king who had set out on the chase noticed his dogs pursuing a white rabbit which was a little ahead of them. When the little rabbit began to sense that the dogs were about to pounce upon him, turning suddenly around, he bounded back quietly and jumped up into the arms of the huntsman. Deeply moved by this show of confidence, the king cherished the rabbit thereafter as his own; he allowed no one to molest him and nourished and cared for the little animal himself.

"This is how God will treat us," Thérèse added, "if, when hunted down by the claims of Divine Justice, represented by the little dogs in the story, we run for refuge into the very arms of our Judge."

Thérèse held out this hope even for the worst sinners on earth: "Ah! I am certain that even if I had on my conscience every imaginable crime, I should lose nothing of my confidence; rather would I hasten into the arms of my Jesus. I remember how he cherished the prodigal son who had returned to him."

Thérèse taught that charity is a precious gold far out-weighing rigorous fasts and penances in God's eyes. She lived an ordinary life with extraordinary awareness that every act done out of love is valued by God; these "trifles", she believed, even please Jesus more than spectacular deeds of holiness. Her love channeled itself into thousands of hidden victories over self: paying exquisite attention to the nuns she liked least, coddling a cantankerous, thankless invalid, relinquishing her precious free time to help another nun, enduring the bone-chilling winter cold in her cell without a word and smiling through all the daily pin pricks of an austere community life. Hour after hour, Thérèse's iron will conquered these challenges, permeating love—like a whiff of perfume—through the stark hallways of the cloister.

Few people realize that Saint Thérèse, usually depicted in statues and paintings with a blissful expression and an armload of fresh roses, suffered a laborious spiritual dryness during most of her convent life. When she arose for morning prayers, or awoke to pray in the night, or attended retreats, the sweet sense of God's presence never greeted her. She was generous enough to realize that prayer is not for satisfying ourselves, but to give pleasure and love to God.

Sometimes, when prayer was particularly tedious, she formulated a mental image of Jesus asleep in her boat, just as he once slept in the boat of the apostle-fisherman Peter; rather than awaken him when the storms of doubt and monotony arose, she let him sleep in peace, trusting that the master of the waves would always be close at hand.

One day Thérèse asked God for a martyrdom of body and soul—suffering in exchange for the rescue of many souls who might not otherwise get safely to heaven. God seemed to honor Thérèse's courageous request for her last months were marked with intense agony. Pulmonary tuberculosis, hemorrhages, gangrene of the intestines, and large painful ulcers reduced her life to constant pain. Far more searing was the immense personal darkness in her spirit—for her last eighteen months on earth were bombarded with temptations and doubts against faith. She actually pinned a copy of the Creed onto the undergarments over her chest, begging God to help her believe. This "dark night of the soul", experienced by some of the saintly giants in history, such as John of the Cross, smothered Thérèse in a kind of crucifixion.

As death approached Thérèse had an urgency to sow the seeds of spiritual childhood in others all over the world. "I want to tell them," she told Mother Agnes, her own older sister Pauline, "that there is only one thing for us to do here below: to throw at Jesus' feet the flowers of little sacrifices, to win him through our caresses. That is the way in which I have taken hold of him, and that is why I shall get such a good welcome."

Close to death, Thérèse had a certainty that she would continue to work for souls and for good from heaven. She frequently told the nuns that she would be with them after her death, that she would never rest but keep helping the Church from heaven until the end of time. In her own words, she promised to let fall from heaven a shower of roses.

"It's not 'death' that will come in search of me, it's God", she once proclaimed. God did come for his little spouse on September 30, 1897 when she was only twenty-four. Thérèse had always insisted that sanctity does not require many years, only much love.

Almost overnight, word of the unusual little Carmelite of Lisieux spread like a great wind over France, then to all of Europe and beyond, a "storm of glory" one Pope would call it. Her autobiography would pass through millions of hands before her canonization only twenty-eight years later.

Mother Agnes had chosen a poem, *Rappelle-Toi*, to be printed on the cross destined for Thérèse's tomb. This original inscription was almost completely effaced when a workman reached for it while the paint was still wet. Considering this an indication of God's will, Mother Agnes had the cross freshly inscribed with Thérèse's own prophecy which still marks it today:

Soeur Thérèse de l'Enfant Jésus 1873–1897
Je veux passer mon ciel a faire du bien sur la terre.
I will spend my heaven doing good on earth.

Nesting

Since we have already written about motherhood in general, this section will focus on the part of the motherly instinct in all women called nesting. Nesting, so named by psychologists, is illustrated most dramatically when a pregnant woman, just before the baby comes, feels almost compelled to fix up the home in preparation for her child's birth. Included in this section about nesting are some quotations on the joys of homemaking and some beautiful thoughts from Marian Women in Ministry.

To be Queen Elizabeth within a definite area deciding sales, banquets, labors, and holidays; . . . providing toys, boots, sheets, cakes, and books; to be Aristotle within a certain area, teaching morals, manners, theology, and hygiene; I can understand how this might exhaust the mind, but I cannot imagine how it could narrow it. How can it be a large career to tell other people's children about the Rule of Three, and a small career to tell one's own children about the universe? How can it be broad to be the same thing to everyone, and narrow to be everything to someone? No; a woman's function is laborious, but because it is gigantic, not because it is minute. I will pity Mrs. Jones for the hugeness of her task; I will never pity her for its smallness.

G. K. Chesterton

Saint Bonaventure said that after the long fast of our Lord in the desert, when the angels came to minister to Him, they went first to the Blessed Mother to see what she had on her stove, and got the soup she had prepared and transported it to our Lord, who relished it the more because his mother had prepared it. Of course.

The trouble is, people do not work in peace and quiet. They bustle, like Martha.

Dorothy Day

To have too much to do is for most safer than to have too little.

Cardinal Manning

The kind of work we do does not make us holy but we may make it holy.

Meister Eckhart

I saw that he is to us everything which is good and comforting for our help. He is our clothing, who wraps and enfolds us, for his love embraces us and shelters us, surrounds us, for his love, which is so tender that he may never desert us.

Julian of Norwich

One of my favorite women is the mother of eleven! Previously a journalist and creative writer, after her conversion to the Catholic Faith she was eager to bring her natural gifts into her new life as a Christian house-wife. I include excerpts here from an article she wrote:

MAKING HOMELIFE
A CREATIVE ADVENTURE

by Marjorie Delaney

Seeking adventure, a man sold his home and bought a boat. He was scarcely out of the harbor with his family when the boat smashed up on the rocks. The poor man lost everything according to the newspaper account because he had had no training in how to sail a boat.

Sailing the boat of family life is just as risky without some knowledge of attitudes and the understanding of what constitutes true adventure, for its spirit colors and creates the emotions. Its secret was casually revealed to me for the first time by an old sea captain. Standing on the boat-dock in San Francisco, our talk had naturally turned to his ninety-six foot schooner, which took college boys down to the South Seas. I remarked, "Every time you stick your head out of the hatch, people in the Midwest like to hear about it. Why don't you write a book about your adventures?"

"No", he declined as he shook the ashes out of his pipe. "Everything has become too commonplace for me. Taking boys on these cruises has made me more like a bus driver. It's really only the traveler making his first voyage who sees it with fresh eyes and can write of its adventures."

The thought challenged me that this man with the romantic looking boat had tired tourist eyes. Here was an adventurer with no adventure. Why standing by the stove, I might have more adventure of soul than the captain. Adventure does not lie in outer physical change. Rather it is experienced on all three levels of being, the physical, the mental, and the spiritual. It was exciting to think that I, as a parent, could set sail from the port of passivity into the great ocean of mystery which is God's Love by deliberately developing adventure as a whole attitude of soul. . . .

The genuine voyager is out on deck to catch the tang of salt air and to revel in the mysteries of the elements. He has his analogy in the type of parent who finds the salt air of problems challenging and purifying by the tang of their demands. For him problems have poetry in eventually revealing the marvels of Providence and the Lord's own Heart.

Adventure is for now and begins with those little practices of bending one's head in the dust like a bicycle tire in order to go forward. Or again, it is by swallowing the pill of pride until one becomes very small and can go through the keyhole of Wonderland like Alice.

Another practice is to keep right at hand on the breakfast table the Bible, a book of poetry, a biology book, or encyclopedia and paying a child for each fifteen minutes with it as well as finding adventure in it oneself or to marvel with the family at meals.

When a child stands in the kitchen saying, "I don't have anything to do", and feels at a standstill, he can be given a few suggestions of course, but a deeper way is to plunge him into the mystery of being and enchant him. For example, one of my daughters followed me around on an afternoon and asked me "why I worked".

I laughed with a twinkle in my eye and said "Work has secrets and I'm finding the secrets."

"What are they", she asked.

"That Christ creates a light around the place you've ordered. That there is a feeling of satisfaction, and even a music to the hour." To this day that particular child seems to enjoy her work and find an adventure in it, all because it was more of an invitation than a command.

It is easy to counteract the spirit of boredom by a calm, confident statement that there is poetry hidden in the pockets of the hours.

Mirroring a calm joy or a spirit of fun nourishes the child and woos him into a relish for life and an attitude of creative anticipation.

The biggest adventures for the parent are the adventures in Grace. Typical of these times was one morning when one of the children told me he had heard me reading through the wall to the smaller children about a saint the night before and that he had experienced an unusual burning in his heart. Later I was thrilled in finding out he had been getting up extra early all summer in order to read the Psalms of David because Divine Grace had drawn him so clearly.

Another moment of adventure happened when my five-year-old was following me around while I was dusting. I noticed he had cotton stuck in his ears. I asked him if he was playing spaceman. "No", he said. "I'm listening to God." It was then that I knew having a heart for adventure meant opening oneself up to the true and the beautiful and to the expectation of the Supernatural Reality in our lives.

Wonder followed upon wonder. When one of my sons was older he stayed up for two nights with a friend who was terribly sick. I found my son on the sofa the next morning in awe having dreamed of the Blessed Mother all in gold with golden rays pouring from her that knocked him off his feet. That very day when a priest called me for a reading during Mass, I found myself reading the passage, "The queen stands at his right hand, arrayed in gold." Adventure is positively linked with one's own inner meaning. These adventures on the doorstep of the day are for us all, to be written down and treasured, even painted if necessary to clothe oneself in adventure as a whole attitude of soul. . . .

Another principle in enjoying an object with loving intensity is to picture the object or person in the original creative idea and even to discover the history. For example, one can see a table with new eyes by re-living the excitement of a man's discovery of the concept and its actuality.

Even a bowl of tomato soup can be dazzling when you think back to the field where a tomato is picked by a woman with tired legs and a child on her back, perhaps a tear from a husband's complaint. To recall the history of the human hands that processed, packed on trucks, and transported the soup, fills the soul with awe and gratitude that so many hands worked to bring the soup "just to me".

This is a secret that some of the greatest and most lasting artists have drawn on in order to pre-dispose themselves to see an object with loving attention and an appreciative eye. In this way the artists see through and beyond the object by re-living its history, the people and their emotions surrounding the image and then deeply feeling the image.

Another major discovery came when I wearily faced a sink full of dishes. Just for fun I found myself thinking of five things about the job to praise God. First, thank God I didn't have to carry water from the well. Secondly, I didn't have to even heat it. Thirdly, my soap was ready made, praise God, I didn't have to stand over a hot vat stirring. Fourth, I was well enough to stand on my own legs and not have to hire a maid. Fifth, praise God, God had given me dishes. By the time I left the kitchen sink I was singing and working energetically.

For in making homelife a creative adventure, the creative parent knows how to bring the house alive with fire, feast, and flowers. She feels the house she lives in to be a symbol of the house of her heart, needing its fire, feast, and flowers also. The fire of the inner house is the motivating line from poetry or Scripture which lights up the darkness. The feast in her heart is more than hot biscuits. It is the wakening awareness of the Divine Energy around her, as she looks out the window to see a schoolboy crossing the street in marvelous balance or a snail crossing the grass, looking regal and lovely as a queen with dew diamonds. Finally, the flowers of the inner house of her heart are those emotional blossoms brought to bloom from positive attitudes. It makes Scripture easy to understand, "Bud forth and blossom like the lily, yield a sweet smell, and bring forth leaves in Grace."

Here are some shorter reflections about meeting God in the midst of the home days.

About gardening, Linda Helminiak writes: "Would that every woman could experience the pleasure and cooperation with God in helping bring to life the seeds planted in the sweet earth. Even if it were just a row of lettuces and radishes, what fulfillment, and the chance for close contemplation of Christ—a beautiful and simple lesson in his Resurrection!"

Anita Hickey thinks that

today many Catholics believe we idealize Mary and are inclined to place her above Christ. I truly feel sorry for these people, for they do not know that Mary's greatest grace is to bring us to an intimate relationship with her Divine Son.

Actually, the contemplative way of life is just that. It brings one to a new, closer, and beautiful relationship with Christ. One need not be reminded of all the many responsibilities we have in our daily lives. However, once we realize how much Christ wants us to be aware of his presence, we can make our many tasks much easier to accomplish. He walks with us through the dishes, cooking, shopping. . . .

Just take a moment to look at his masterpiece of life. He is present in all if we take the time to look for him. Begin each day with a quiet time devoted just to him. Listen deep within your soul and he will let his presence be felt. He is truly a marvelous friend, but be prepared for surprises, for he is a mystery, and one must be willing to walk in darkness at times. He may be silent, but he is there.

Part of the joy of homemaking is the cultivation of simplicity. Pope John Paul II implores us to fulfill the gospel by living in a "simple and austere" way. He is not addressing his remarks to the poor who are bound to live with a certain simplicity, but mainly to the middle class and wealthy. Many of us in the middle-income bracket feel strapped at the end of the month and therefore develop a psychology of poverty, and yet if we would dare to count up all the items in our houses we would probably find that they number in the ten thousands! Shame!

Since beginning Marian Women in Ministry, the Lord has put in my path many women who are being converted to simplicity as a part of their Christian lifestyle. Following Saint Paul in 1 Thessalonians 5, they want to hold on to what is good and avoid every form of evil—luxury and waste being seen as evils.

It can become a stimulating hobby to figure out what is for the good and what is over-collecting. One woman I know decided to get rid of most of her clothing and dress simply in a few blue skirts (she is a Marian Woman) and sweaters, with a very fancy white blouse and skirt for going out. To her surprise no one noticed the difference! But she felt freed from preoccupation with her appearance. Another woman gave up pillows—after one night of awkwardness, she found her arm would do just as well. Another gave up fancy shampoos and soaps for the cheapest kind. One woman gives away whatever she finds in her closets which she hasn't used in an entire year. Giving up the second car and doing more walking can be refreshing for those whose need for the second car is more habitual than truly obligatory.

Of course, it is not Christian to make any of these forms of simplicity into absolutes or to insist that others follow. According to Saint Francis de Sales, who helped develop lay spirituality, a person living in the world has a right to possess whatever is good for carrying out his duties and using his talents. A $1,000 cello which would be a luxury for a dilettante musician would be a necessity for a professional musician.

An idea coming from feminism which might help you discern your own path to simplicity is that a woman should try to develop her own style rather than clinging to formalities out of insecurity.

Why not ask the Holy Spirit to lead you to the simplicity most suited to your own growth and the real needs of those around you? The women I know who have tried find that this process is not penance but sheer joy!

I'm sure Mary was all simplicity!

Intimacy in Friendship

Love of friends is certainly not an exclusively feminine gift. Some of the most beautiful lines about friendship have been written by men!

Rightly has a friend been called "the half of my soul".

Augustine quoting Aristotle

The essence of a perfect friendship is that each friend reveals himself utterly to the other, flings aside his reserves and shows himself for what he truly is.

R. H. Benson

Without a friend, it is as if the sun is taken from the sky.

Saint Peter Canisius

It would prove to be a very happy afternoon if you were to sit down quietly and remember the whole tale of your friendships throughout your whole life. You can thank God for those who have been lost on earth through death or separation and also thank the friends you now have present by means of a phone call or a letter.

Many friendships, same sex and opposite sex, are all joy. But some of those of the greatest intensity are fraught with problems. A leaflet I wrote for Dove a few years ago has helped many people to understand what is happening in such spiritual friendships and so I am including it here.

STAGES IN SPIRITUAL FRIENDSHIP

In the course of many workshops I have given in the area of spirituality, the topic of spiritual friendship comes to the fore. I am quite astounded at the intensity of the questions raised by participants. This has caused me to try to develop a well-rounded teaching on this delicate but timely subject.

Catholics familiar with the lives of the saints know of the beautiful friendships which existed between such holy men and women as Saint Francis and Saint Clare, Saint Teresa of Avila and Gracian, Saint Francis de Sales and Saint Jane de Chantal, Saint Benedict and his sister.

Most probably we also know of cases where seemingly holy people of our acquaintance, or we ourselves, have gone off the deep end in pursuit of such companionship.

We wonder whether we are truly holy enough to sustain intimate friendship of the particular fervency characteristic of spiritual union. We may wonder if others under our direction, or those who come to us for advice, are mature enough to develop such relationships without danger.

In the development of guidelines in this sensitive area, it is helpful to delineate some of the common stages such friendships might pass through. After so doing we will be able to assess where we ourselves or others are in the process of discernment.

Stage One: Attraction. How often we meet people in our church associations who are devout, loving, with much in common, and yet we feel no special desire to get closer to them! But from time to time we meet a person of the opposite or same sex, the same age, younger or older, in whom we sense some special spiritual beauty. We want to get to know this individual because we sense that his or her qualities have some affinity with our own goals.

Stage Two: Mutuality. Sometimes a friendship never goes past Stage One. We admire someone intensely, but there is no sign that this person feels any desire to get closer to us. But other times the gift is given. We are delighted to discover that a human being who seems to us so wonderful, so in touch with God, has been given the grace to see through all our shortcomings to the core of what God has given us of his beauty. Generally, when the gift of mutuality is given, circumstances making it possible, the two seek out each other's company, enjoying not only the sharing of prayer, but also the unfolding of the personality which comes from feeling loved and cherished.

Stage Three: Enchantment. Some very solid, enduring spiritual friendships skip over this marvelous but tormenting stage to go right on to a peaceful tender union in Stage Four. But many who embark on the course of intimacy find themselves either passing through the stage of enchantment or getting stuck in what have been called the toxic parts of intoxication.

It is impossible to see the beauty of another person's spirit without wanting in some way to possess that quality. What we want, however, is not a disembodied characteristic, but the particular wonderful trait as embodied in this individual.

It *is* possible to be one with another spiritually, but precisely when we renounce possessing them emotionally or physically. Since we are used to trying to possess things physically and emotionally, we find it a terrible strain to be deprived of this normal type of closeness.

To be more concrete, you can possess an ice cream cone by eating it. We can possess a wife or husband by entering into a commitment as in marriage, 'til death do us part. But in a spiritual friendship you are not allowed to have the other physically.

Some Christians try for a compromise here. Of course they know that sexual intercourse is a serious mortal sin, but they think they can derive erotic joy from less complete contacts. I believe that such a path is full of self-deception. Any touching different from the affection all Christians should display (which can be viewed by any stranger without suspicion) always carries an erotic charge, distracting from the spiritual nature of the union, and often leading to more complete acts.

Spiritual friendship should be an eschatological sign of the union we will experience in heaven, which will be complete but not erotic, as we are told by the Lord. In fact, a foretaste on earth of the physical yet non-sensual fulfillment depends on renunciation.

Emotional possession is also contrary to the meaning of spiritual friendship. What do I mean by emotional possession? In marriage, in parenting, in a religious community, others have a right to a priority position in their claim on our time and energy. In a friendship this is not the case. To neglect the family, or the community, because of the greater delight of being with a spiritual friend is to violate the primary duty of love which comes from our chosen state of life. This means that a spiritual friend cannot make inordinate demands on the other. The time together should be a gift, not something obligatory.

Now, many Christians, no matter how spiritual they may be, have the greatest difficulty accepting the transcendent character of such friendships. Impelled by terrific longings for physical and emotional fulfillment, they will find themselves in a state of torment when such possession is denied them.

In such cases the choice may present itself of sin, suicide, or an abrupt and excruciating termination of the friendship.

Let us say a few words about each of these possibilities. It is not a sin to be the prey of fantasies of sexual union. It is sinful purposely to indulge in these or to plan concretely to carry them out, or to engage in physical acts of an intimate kind. Most healthy spiritual friendships pass through a phase of temptation along these lines, but a good one goes beyond this to a peaceful sense of temperate self-control. Quantitatively, much more of the time with a spiritual partner or in inner dialogue should be spent in prayer and deep conversation than in longing for physical union.

It is important that each participant in a spiritual friendship have a director other than the friend who can discern if such temptations are getting out of hand and if termination may be essential to preserve one or the other or both from falling into serious sin.

Thoughts or words such as, "I will die if I cannot be with my friend as lover, community member, wife, husband"—when previous commitments or purity rule these possibilities out of the question—indicate an idol-worship relationship which is a serious offense to God who alone is our Savior. Oftentimes psychological as well as spiritual counseling is necessary to begin to heal the wounds of the past which underlie such desperate need to possess any loved person.

As indicated above, in some cases one or both parties in spiritual friendship do not go through the painful Stage Three (enchantment) but move right on to Stage Four.

Stage Four: Union. Here we come to an intense but nonetheless tranquil experience of oneness. Two spirits, previously distinct, begin to blend. During prayer, together or apart, such spiritual friends can possess Christ at the same moment with ecstatic joy or delightful contentment.

Very often one will be able to know what is going on in the heart of the other even without words. Most efficacious intercession is possible at Stage Four where there are no more barriers of distrust and fear. When one partner is down the other will be able to find just the right words to lead him into the Heart of Christ.

A clear mark of union is unselfish desire to share the beloved with others. Characteristically, a married person gifted with spiritual companionship with another outside the marriage will find that his spousal union is getting closer. Feelings of disappointment and resentment give way to a happy gratitude for the gifts the spouse is able to give. The sense of bond with the marriage partner or with other friends, members of a community or children, grows as through the gifts of spiritual friendship the soul expands in its ability to read the hearts of others.

As many writers have shown, much inner healing comes

from such union. As confidence develops in the unconditional love of such a friend, previous fears of rejection and abandonment begin to diminish. Hidden talents, buried due to the neutrality or harsh criticism of authority figures of the past, begin to emerge in the new atmosphere of loving reverence built up by spiritual union.

For these reasons we find spiritual friendship to be one of the greatest gifts of God in this life, worth striving for and cherishing.

A final point about friendships which are aborted before arriving at the safe harbor of Stage Four. Though the experience is extremely painful, we still gain much from an unhappy attempt at spiritual friendship. Our heart opens wide in sympathy for rejections undergone by others who come to us for help. We receive insight of a most penetrating kind about the way in which Christ is wounded by our unwillingness to open to the grace of love *he* wants to extend to *us* in our suspicious closedness. Often a troubled friendship is a stage on the way to a future, more mature, successful one.

O God, you will that we love you with our whole hearts, minds, and all our strength, and our neighbor as ourselves. Grant us the gift of the experience of your absolute, all-fulfilling love, and, as you will for us, the further gift of pure union in you with the brothers and sisters you have chosen for us. Amen.

I think that many of us have wonder in our hearts at the thought of what the spiritual friendship of Mary and Joseph must have been like. Here is a lovely description written by a Marian Woman:

THE QUIET MAN . . .

Mary Remembers, as the Day of Resurrection Draws Near

by Mary Dorothy Walsh

Joseph labored slowly and with dexterity. The lamp stand was almost finished. He had worked on it for days in his spare time. It must be just right. The wood responded to his skilled hands as he carved. He was smiling to himself and singing an old Hebrew folk song in hushed tones. The young man thought of the beautiful girl who would be his wife. Mary. It was for her, this gift of love. He stood back and scrutinized the table. Just a few more touches and it would be finished. It had to be just right. Mary would be so pleased with it. She was such a joy—so easy to satisfy. Joseph knew she would appreciate all the hours and affection that went into this very special betrothal present. He could hardly wait to bring it to her—to see her eyes light up with gratitude and pride in the work of the man to whom she was engaged. Joseph marveled in thought at his good fortune to have such a jewel as Mary love and respect this lowly carpenter.

Joseph was a good, law-abiding Jew. He observed the Commandments, attended synagogue faithfully and performed the rituals proper to him. His reputation was impeccable. A carpenter by trade, Joseph was known for his honesty in the marketplace and for the quality of his goods. He was just in all his dealings. Kindness and compassion toward neighbor and stranger alike distinguished him. The truth was that any young Jewess would have been pleased to be the bride of Joseph of Nazareth. However, Joseph in his meekness could not see the sterling qualities of his own nature. His devotion to Yahweh was such that all his thoughts, words and actions were directed to pleasing the Most High. From this attitude on his part came his holiness of life. In turn, that holiness won for Joseph the honor of being chosen as husband of Mary. Who could doubt that God would choose as guardian and protector for his Mother, the man most worthy. The legal father of the Son of God would be Joseph. Had he realized that Yahweh favored him with such trust, his humility would have over-whelmed him with reluctance. It was better that he didn't know—yet.

In thought, Joseph went back to the day in the Temple when he had been summoned along with all the young eligible men of the house of David. Upon arrival the High Priest announced that it was time for the maiden Mary to choose a husband. Mary was from the family of David and Jewish law mandated marriages to be contracted within one's own tribe hence Joseph's good fortune to be in the select group of prospective husbands. And the lot had fallen to him! How could he be worthy of such a blessing, such favor from God! Little did the young man realize that his faithfulness in the little everyday duties of life had resulted in his designation as provider and guardian for the Redeemer of the world and his virgin Mother.

Joseph laid his tools aside now. He was tired after a long day in the shop. Stepping outside, he raised his eyes to the star-studded canopy stretching across the land of Judah. How good life seemed! Heartfelt prayers of praise and gratitude reverberated again in his soul. In just a few short months—or would it seem forever in coming!—Mary would enter his home to share his life. And together they would worship the one True God. Joseph had learned that Mary's heart too was set on the Lord and observing his ways. They would live under the gaze of the Almighty Yahweh giving him the homage of first place all the days of their lives. Tomorrow he would bring the lamp stand, his gift, to his beloved.

Mary's eyes searched Joseph's as she spoke. She loved this gentle, shy, quiet man dearly. The more she came to know him during their acceptable times together, the more she

admired him.—Could she expect or hope he would understand and believe what she was telling him? Their engagement
gave Joseph almost the privileges of a husband, the right to
know what concerned his future wife was his by law. They
had already shared secrets of their hearts including that which
concerned their vows of virginity. This secret too, mighty as it
was, had to be divulged only to this man.—Mary was with
child. And all she could say at this point was that they must
trust God and that she had not betrayed him.

Joseph stood looking up at the sky. It was dark and angry
looking—the brilliance of the preceding night, like the joy of
his heart, gone now. The wind was picking up as lightning
flashed. Then the crash of thunder! It began to rain. Drops of
the heaven-sent moisture mingled with the tears on the young
carpenter's upturned face. His heart ached. It broke. What
should he do? What could he do? What wisdom would en-
lighten his heavy spirit and lead him to the right decision, a
decision only he must make? Still scanning the firmament, that
heaven from which he believed his help would come, he
prayed aloud beseeching Yahweh for the guidance he sorely
needed. But the words were drowned out by the fury of the
sudden storm.

Joseph had taken the lamp stand to Mary and learned from
her that she was pregnant, yet had not betrayed his love. And
she was going to Ain Karim to stay with her aged cousin
Elizabeth who was expecting a child. Mary would not return
for three months. It was a lot for anyone to comprehend
clearly. His betrothed mysteriously pregnant; Elizabeth, old
beyond the normal time of conception, also pregnant and
Mary leaving Nazareth to be of service to her. Joseph realized
that by the time of her return, Mary's pregnancy would be
obvious. Then her life would be in danger; the Law prescribed
stoning in such a case. Joseph also knew that he could never
allow his beautiful, good Mary to be subjected to the scorn of

the village nor to the rigors of the custom. She would not be exposed publicly. No, though it would break his heart anew, Joseph would take the only way possible and send his beloved away privately.

Mary returned from Ain Karim. During her absence, Joseph had agonized constantly over the situation. True, his decision was made but tormenting thoughts went through his mind. Passage of time neither quieted his uneasiness nor dimmed his love for the young maiden. Unanswered questions gave him anguish yet he dared not seek relief through confiding in anyone. He had to remain quiet to protect Mary. To God alone did Joseph have recourse. Only he knew of the sufferings he was permitting his trusted servant to endure. Only he could put an end to them. Joseph in his patience presented a calm exterior to the villagers. While noticing his preoccupation, they attributed it to the coming wedding.

The heaviness in Joseph's heart had reached an unbearable state. He was in such conflict. His decision to send Mary away divorcing her quietly wrestled constantly with his loving attachment to her. How could he bear to part with her? Yet it had to be and now that she was back he would have to tell her. He knelt in prayer before retiring for still another night of broken, uneasy slumber. Falling into a deep sleep, Joseph had a dream. "Joseph, son of David, have no fear about taking Mary as your wife. It is by the Holy Spirit that she has conceived this Child. She is to have a Son and you are to name him Jesus because he will save his people from their sins" (Mt 1:20–21), thus spoke the Angel of the Lord.

Joseph woke with the light of dawn. There was no doubt in his mind but that the dream was the answer to his prayers. His heart was fairly bursting with joy! Mary was completely justified. The Angel had commanded Joseph to go and receive Mary as his wife and obediently he would do so. He did not understand—but he believed. The ways of the Most High were unsearchable and often shrouded in mystery. The circumstances of his bride's pregnancy would be known to the couple alone until some future time which God would reveal.

Thirty-three years had slipped by since Mary had gone to share Joseph's home and be a part of his life. With the birth of her Son several months after the wedding, their joy had been complete. Joseph, whose legal right it was to name the Child, had called him Jesus. For he was to save his people from their sins. He had just accomplished that act of redemption.

Mary held her Jesus, just taken down from the cross, tenderly in her arms. Quiet tears streamed down her still beautiful face and fell on his lifeless body. Gently she touched the bruised cheeks and swollen lips. The countenance, which so resembled her own, was now disfigured beyond recognition. The executioners had spared no part of him; welts and lacerations covered his features. Her Son's corpse was almost one vast wound.

Holding Jesus in death, Mary remembered another loved one with whom she also had parted. Her gentle, humble Joseph as uncomplaining in suffering as his foster Son, had died in her arms years earlier. She felt his quiet presence in spirit giving her strength through the hours that she stood beneath the cross watching their beloved Jesus dying in agony. She felt Joseph beside her still as now she prepared Jesus for burial. They hurried to place him in the new sepulchre which belonged to a friend from Arimathea. It was growing dark.

Mary watched as a huge stone was set in place across the entrance of the tomb. Widowed and with no other child to comfort her, the Mother left the cemetery. Heart sundered, her full faith in the promise of Jesus to rise from the dead could not allay the depth of her sorrow. Forever she would remember the sight of his pain-racked face as he struggled for hours on the cross before of his own accord, Jesus gave up his spirit.—Had she ever forgotten the sufferings of Joseph? Yet with her husband, she had been able to give comfort and succor.—No, some memories are too cruel ever to fade.—

Mary slowly made her way down the hill of Calvary. Mankind had been redeemed—and at what a purchase price! The Mother had paid her share of it. She felt that Joseph, the quiet husband of her marriage years, long gone to a place beyond all sorrow, knew it. This thought consoled her. O Mary, the Resurrection is soon to come.

With that great dawn, rejoicing will be yours!

The Joyful Mysteries of the Rosary

1. *The Annunciation:* Mary learns from the Angel Gabriel that God wishes her to be the mother of God and humbly accepts (Lk 1:26–38).

2. *The Visitation:* Mary goes to visit her cousin Elizabeth and is praised by her as "blessed among women" (Lk 1:39–56).

3. *The Nativity:* Mary gives birth to Jesus in the stable at Bethlehem (Lk 2:1–20).

4. *The Presentation:* Mary and Joseph present Jesus to his Heavenly Father in the Temple of Jerusalem forty days after his birth (Lk 2:22–39).

5. *The Finding in the Temple:* After searching for three days, Mary and Joseph find the twelve-year-old Jesus sitting in the Temple discussing the law with the learned doctors (Lk 2:42–52).

Meditation on the Joyful Mysteries of the Rosary is recommended for Mondays and Thursdays and for Sundays during Advent. Instruction on praying the rosary can be found on page 197.

The

Sorrowful Mysteries

Of Being a Woman

Womanly Suffering

To introduce the sorrowful mysteries of being a woman, here are a few quotations on suffering to give context to the sorrows particular to us.

Even though you may for a short time have to bear being plagued by all sorts of trials, so that when Jesus Christ is revealed your faith will have been tested and proved like gold. . . .

1 Peter 1:6–7

You must consider that every state of life is in some way irksome, bitter, and unpleasant. . . . The Everlasting God has in his wisdom foreseen from eternity the cross that he now presents to you as a gift from his inmost Heart. This cross he now sends you he has considered with his all knowing eyes, understood with his divine mind, tested with his wise justice, warmed with loving arms and weighed with his own hands to see that it be not one inch too large and not one ounce too heavy for you. He has blessed it with his holy Name, anointed it with his grace, perfumed it with his consolation, taken one last glance at you and your courage, and then sent it to you from heaven, a special greeting from God to you, an alms of the all-merciful love of God.

Francis de Sales

To the world which could care less, comes him who could not care more.

Msgr. T. O'Sullivan

Let nothing trouble thee, let nothing afright thee, all things pass away, God never changes, patience obtains everything, God alone suffices.

Teresa of Avila

The storm is like the cry of some God in pain whose love the earth refuses.

Tagore

Some of my reflections on suffering may be of help to you. When I try to meet Christ in suffering, I always come back to an experience of many years ago. It was in Mexico City where I saw a man kneeling in prayer before a very realistic life-size crucifix. The poor and pained man stretched out his arms, his lips moving in silent prayer, his eyes fixed on the figure of Christ. So he was when I entered the church and so he remained for more than half an hour. Finally, with a sort of nod of mutual understanding to his Jesus, he left, not joyful but at peace.

What struck me was the purity of this man's identification of his own suffering with that of Christ. By contrast I often begin to deal with pain by petitions, move on to bribes: "If I add these prayers each day . . . will you take away this cross?" Then anger and murmuring if my will is not done. Finally, exhausted from "twisting" on the cross, I give up and beg God to help me carry it more grace-fully. What helps is if, much earlier in the process, I happen to pass a picture of Christ and realize that my cross is his cross. Then I can place my wounded head into his wounded hands and let him heal me, or rest my weary body in the lap of Mary, that she might soothe me. Then I see that to suffer with him is better than to be without crosses far from him. I can pray, again, for the removal of the cross, with peace, hope, and confidence in his loving will instead of desperate fear. Meditating on the Stations of the Cross is a great help also in identifying my sufferings with his. May I suggest that, right now, you stop reading this and bring your heaviest cross to him for his comfort? Think of when your special suffering of loneliness as a single, a widow, a separated or divorced woman, an unhappily married woman; or your suffering of anxiety over your children, or your fear of the death of loved ones was felt by Jesus or Mary on earth or now in the Mystical Body.

The Stations of the Cross

1. Jesus is condemned to death.
2. Jesus carries his Cross.
3. Jesus falls the first time.
4. Jesus meets his Mother.
5. Jesus is helped by Simon of Cyrene.
6. Veronica wipes the face of Jesus.
7. Jesus falls a second time.
8. Jesus speaks to the women.
9. Jesus falls a third time.
10. Jesus is stripped of his clothes.
11. Jesus is nailed to the Cross.
12. Jesus dies on the Cross.
13. Jesus is taken down from the Cross.
14. Jesus is placed in the tomb.

The Sufferings
of the Body

The Menstrual Cycle

For most women, the first experience of sufferings specifically feminine is the onset of the menstrual period. For some this is simple and discomforting, but not very painful; but for many the unpleasantness is compounded by quite a bit of pain. For still others the pain is so excruciating that it entails heavy medication and bed rest.

Many women are also subject to moodiness based on the times of the cycle. Unawareness of the cause of this can increase bewilderment and irritation.

Then later, for mothers, come the troubles of pregnancy—nausea, heaviness, and childbirth itself, followed by the fatigue of caring for babies and toddlers. For most, in spite of the joys, this is overwhelmingly exhausting.

What will follow are some ways to alleviate these sufferings and to meet Christ in them.

Sister Mary Ann Follmar bases this analysis of the menstrual cycle on the book *Psychosexual Functions*, by Therese Benedek:

THE CYCLE OF WOMAN

The body of woman possesses a dynamic potency which allows her to prepare a home for life and, at the same time, to grow in the spiritual life. A woman, ordinarily, is in a cycle for about thirty-five years of her life and experiences within herself the rhythm of ascent and descent. Though the usual reference for the cycle is physiological, the rhythm of the cycle colors the entire fabric of a woman's life whether she is conscious of this encompassing feature or oblivious of it. Due to the unity of the human person, all the aspects of her life are inter-dependent. Hence spiritually, creatively, physically, and emo-tionally a woman is in cycle.

During the proliferative phase of the cycle the secretion of estrogen increases. The estrogen build-up is frequently ac-companied by a feeling of well-being and alertness as well as a more active heterosexual drive. Physically, the sense of well-being and energy of the sexual drive can stimulate a woman to engage in activities which exercise and invigorate her body. Intellectually, this can be the time for research or play with ideas. Spiritually, a similar zest may be present resulting in eagerness to help the Body of Christ to grow through the gift of self. Emotionally, if the heterosexual drive has been directed positively, a woman knows a refreshing serenity. The secretion of estrogen which has the latter effects, attains its peak at ovulation, the time when progesterone production is initiated. Progesterone increases the capacity and desire of a woman to enter into union. The heightened sense of vitality and the desire for union may cause a woman physically to spring into action; intellectually and creatively to pour forth in composi-tion the fruitfulness of insights; spiritually, to be enflamed by the fire of the Spirit and to enter with gratitude into deeper union with the Body of Christ. In contrast, ovulation may be a time of intense suffering for a woman who desires union and feels that desire thwarted. However, whatever a woman feels during this time can be directed and become a means toward spiritual growth.

During the secretory or progestational phase a woman tends to be more calm and self-possessed in the sense of preparing herself to nourish and provide a home for other persons. During this phase a woman may thirst to share ideas and creatively plan how to collaborate with other persons. This yearning can stimulate her to be sensitive to the needs, the ideas and the expressions of others. Spiritually, this may be the time of longing to enter into the work of community worship. The final days of the progestational phase form the pre-menstrual phase during which time hormone production diminishes. The hormone variations are expressed, at times, in tenseness, irritability, impatience, frustration, and depression. Physically, due to the decreased production of estrogen and the cessation of progesterone, a woman can be quite fatigued. This physical state can be accompanied by aridity, boredom or even hatred for prayer because of a sense of isolation and incapacity for union. Intellectually it may seem, now, that the power of thought has withered leaving a person barren and incapable of synthesizing ideas or of developing thought. A woman may even be overwhelmed by her lack of knowledge and desire to destroy that which she has developed. Emotion-ally, there may be a feeling of worthlessness or of despair resulting in a riot of destructive desires. A woman may then simply wish to be alone and be repulsed by an embrace or a kiss. However, the sense of barrenness during premenstruation can dispose a woman to perceive more clearly and to draw near to the source of warmth and richness—the Lord Jesus. Then, this phase of her cycle becomes a time of gift.

Once menstruation begins, the tense mood is usually relaxed. This change is accompanied by relief from depression and hostility. With the beginning of a new cycle there may be present in a woman a feeling of springtime and joy at the privilege it offers of entering through the new cycle into greater union and fruitfulness. Thus, there can be during menstruation tranquility of body and soul. A woman may at this time experience great freedom of spirit and readiness for the pursuit of truth. However, it is important to realize that each woman does not respond in the same manner during the different phases of the cycle. Within a particular woman, moreover, the responses may differ somewhat from cycle to cycle since particular events contribute varied nuances to the phases of the cycle. Accordingly, it is not wise for a woman to pre-determine what her response should be, but, rather, to give herself to the endeavor of creatively directing in a positive manner the responses which are present.

Though each woman has her own rhythm within which there are variations, the essential fact is that every woman who is in a cycle knows the sense of death and resurrection from within herself. The cycle, moreover, is not a dead-end repetition but can be a spiral which permits a woman to enter into progressively richer dimensions of union and fruitfulness as she seeks in each new cycle to respond to the rhythm of her being. As she directs her pain and her joy in a creative manner she is able to grow spiritually through these varied experiences.

Because the cycle is part of a woman's life for so many years, I think it important to include a few more women's voices about their experience, especially because I found them quite startling:

> I had begrudged the struggle of the menstruation cycle from the moment I began to experience it. Did not woman suffer enough, my Lord?
>
> Some time ago, at the onset of my monthly routine which included severe abdominal pain, I cried out to the Lord "Why, God, did you make woman this way?"

Ever so quiet, so gentle, his response came: "In order that you may bear and give life."

My Lord's words to me that day were truly life giving. I embraced what had previously been no life, but pain and struggle, and through acceptance of woman as I am, the pains have ceased, and life-giver I choose to be always as he calls to me.

I feel like a full moon when I have my period. when the moon is in its full glory, it changes the flow of many things on the earth: the tide of the ocean, crops in the fields.

The moon is my femininity; the earth, my body with its hormones and moods. Yes, I feel at this moment like a moon in full glory.

Pregnancy and Childbirth

Women experience pregnancy in several different ways. There are a few who find the whole process utterly delightful. It is a time to praise the Lord for all phases of the growth of the baby in the shelter of the womb.

Others go through mild discomfort, anxiety, and depression. It is beneficial to offer up these feelings, uniting them to the Cross of Christ, for intentions such as the health and salvation of the baby.

Some of us suffer through each childbirth much more deeply. Physical disorders can complicate pregnancy with extreme tiredness or depression making care for other family members almost impossible. It should be a time for deep abandonment to God and also for being vulnerable in begging for help of others who are called to grow themselves by not taking wife or mother for granted.

It is very important to look into natural methods of childbirth, home-delivery, and breast-feeding, for these can help alleviate the pain and fatigue associated with childbirth and infant care. I highly recommend reading *How to Be Happy and Holy in Your Own Home* by Deborah Grumbine for complete details on how to enjoy these methods. Here I want to include a description of a home birth I witnessed:

> Last year, I witnessed the nativity in the form of a woman in labor whose childbirth I was allowed to watch. My friend, Elasah Drogin, was to have a delivery at the home of her midwife and close friend, Ann Govan a full-time nurse in a maternity ward.
>
> To be honest, I was not eager to come and witness the event. My own childbearings were far from idyllic. In spite of all the instructions of natural childbirth experts, I shrieked through my short labors. Might not my friend Elasah, a tense type like me, also react as I had done? Thus I hoped that the call inviting me to the home delivery would find me out of the house.
>
> But as Providence would have it, I was home when the call came. What I witnessed at that delivery will probably be the closest I will ever get to knowing what Mary's birthing of Christ was like. Elasah, in her travail, taught

me what it means to suffer as a Christian, in a state of grace, penitentially.

With each contraction, Elasah's face remained undistorted but her eyes became deeper and deeper, more accepting of the penance of childbearing. None of my furious rebellion! She knew that pain is the price of life and she would pay it to the full.

Surrounding her, we sang and prayed aloud. Could Joseph of the chanting Jewish people have done less? Why do we imagine that he felt out of place and fussed with the animals instead of being intimately involved in this terrible but exquisite moment?

Then came the last push. Under the patient guidance of the midwife's hands, the little baby's head came sliding out. Miraculously, there he was: Peter Nicholas Drogin!

Other Womanly Sufferings

As a woman grows older she has an opportunity to think of her body in a new way. Here is one woman's perceptions:

> I feel my body decreasing in strength, the strength I have always known, but increasing in the strength I never knew.
>
> People say "you don't look fifty-eight, you look much younger." I want to say to them: "I want to look fifty-eight." I don't want you feeling bad that I'm fifty-eight. I love being where I am in my journey. I do mind the pain of illness, but I know that in the pain I become aware of a powerful life energy in me that heals my shortness of breath, and when the time comes to let go of breath, of

my wrists, my body, I know I will still be there. That life energy is me.

I am and I always will be and that is life and that is what I feel in my feet climbing mountains and my heart beating. I am the life that God gave me. Someday I will let go of what I don't need, just as I let go of carbon dioxide and waste. I will let go of my body but I will go on walking with the Lord, with brothers and sisters. So, I say, blessed are those who can see a life energy that is greater than any other energy.

What I experience is being considered an old woman, which means an old body—wrinkles, sagging breasts, stomach protruding. Sometimes it is experienced with scorn by another, or in apologetic way—"but you have wisdom". But I *want* to have the body of an old woman, because I am an old woman and I want my body to speak who I am.

At all ages we fight against what we are. Children want to be older and teenagers want to be older, . . . and so we miss what we are. We still need to accept these rejected parts of our journey. At some time we have to accept who we are. It is a deep pain to hate your body at different phases of its life—to hate your period or your pregnancy. It is a gift to come to the point of saying, I like it just the way I am.

This humorous selection from Marian Woman Lois Donahue comes from her delightfully funny book *Dear Moses. . . . Letters to Saints and Other Prominent People*:

Why did I make myself so miserable [by deciding on a diet]? Good question? Well, originally I had a choice— either the self-imposed suffering of diet and exercise or a mentally deteriorating guilt complex inflicted by a society more tolerant of obscenity than obesity. Basically lazy, devoid of will power and incompatible with pain, I decided to go with guilt. I figured I could pass the buck and blame my pudginess on my kids. The way I see it, if I can be held responsible for every one of their major or minor abnormalities, the least they can do in return is shoulder the burden of my figure imperfections. (After all, it only amounts to about five or ten pounds apiece!)

GERMAINE OF PIBRAC

by Dana Black

Here is the story of a little known saint we discovered in our search through the church library for bedtime stories. All of us were deeply touched by this saint, even our fifteen year old son.

Saint Germaine of Pibrac was born about 1579 in a village near Toulouse, France. Her mother died while she was still a toddler. Her father seemed to have no way with small children, so Germaine lived in a world of limited love. When his second marriage came about, Germaine was destined to sink even lower into the depths of the unwanted and unloved. The new stepmother, seeing Germaine's hand withered with deformity understood immediately that this child would be of no worth about the house. . . . Her selfish stepmother, not recognizing a heart of Christ in a broken child, banished her to live in the

---

Saint Germaine is exemplary for her patient endurance through physical and emotional suffering, and the transformation of these bad experiences into good through love of God.

stable, clothed in rags and subsisting on table scraps or a bit of bread. As the pressures of home and family life increased with each new baby, her stepmother began to vent her aggressions on Germaine. She was to endure verbal lashings, physical beatings, and false accusations.

Many of us, were we placed in such a dismal situation at so tender and vulnerable an age, might admit that we would turn bitter under the scalpel of cruelty cutting into our heart. However, our little saint was extraordinarily blessed with an abundance of supernatural grace and revelation. She turned in her misery to God. It was because she did not quiver in the battle of life's trials that she was able to march in the victory procession in heaven. Rather than malice, envy, and slander, she turned to God and her world with overpowering love. It was love that made her a saint, not miracles and raptures. The miracles were only a side effect of Divine Love, like a rainbow shining in the sun after the storm.

Germaine had a spiritual approach to living. Upon moving into the stable, she made a wooden cross with two sticks and a rag. Her bed was gathered up straw. The villagers heard heavenly music and followed ethereal voices to Germaine's barn. They found her kneeling in prayer before the wooden cross, swept in rapture and bathed in golden lights. Imagine the gift of intimacy her soul shared with our Lord.

At daybreak she would receive her minimal rations, her spinning work and her sheep to tend, and journey into the fields. This was dangerous work because of the wolves. When the church bells beckoned her heart to Mass, she would place her distaff in the ground and commend her sheep to the protection of her guardian angel. One particular day the river was swollen with waters from a storm. Alarmed, the village children called out to Germaine not to cross the river. Our Father's will was that she attend Mass, and so he quietly parted the river so that his beloved might safely pass. After Mass

Saint Germaine would always stop to pray at the little altar of our Lady. Her favorite prayer was the rosary, prayed on a small knotted string. This child never learned to read, so her prayers were very simple. She is an inspiration, living in a world over-burdened with intellect and barren in faith.

After Mass, our saint would teach young children and beggars about the love of God. She would also share her small rations with them. Her stepmother became furious when she heard of this. At one point, she publicly beat her until she fell down in agony. As she fell, the apron clasped to her chest opened to reveal a bouquet of spring flowers in winter. This wonder broke through her stepmother's hard heart. She repented and invited Germaine into her home as a family member. Germaine's prayers had been answered. Her stepmother was converted to love. But she preferred her simple life of union with Christ in the stable. She died young, surrounded by angels. May we join in her prayer: "O Lord, I am not worthy of you. Come into my heart and soul and mind, guide my every thought, word and deed."

The Sufferings
of the Heart

This chapter in the sorrowful mysteries of being a woman will deal with many different kinds of suffering. I will speak of meeting Christ in rejection, particularly the rejection we experience within ministry settings, in loneliness, and also in the face of more severe problems.

The Sorrows of Rejection and Loneliness

It is my conviction that most women respond in a different way than most men to feeling rejected. Many men, when confronted with opposition, get angry, but instead of taking it personally, they swiftly assign the blame to the idiocy of their opponents. By contrast, many women take every setback as a personal rejection and experience extreme anguish as a result.

How are we to meet Christ in rejection, especially of the type that occurs within ministry? How can we avoid drowning in self-pity, or becoming corroded with bitterness, or falling into the temptation to withdraw from involvement?

"Clothe yourselves, all of you, with humility toward

one another, for 'God opposes the proud, but gives grace to the humble.' Humble yourselves therefore under the mighty hand of God, that in due time he may exalt you" (1 Pet 5:5–11).

Here are some stages that I go through when I feel rejected. Perhaps reading about them may help you.

My first reaction is sharp pain. When analyzing myself, I find that having had a very happy early childhood, I have a strong expectation that I should receive affirming love from everyone, even those who would be my natural enemies on ideological grounds. This desire for constant love has its good points, because I tend to be more outward-going than those who expect rejection. On the other hand, I have come to see that there is a girlish naiveté in my stance, which needs to be corrected by Christian realism.

My second reaction to rejection is to paint in my mind the most awful caricature of my opponent possible. I find the most sarcastic phrases with which to depict my "enemy", and savor the fantasy of situations in which I could hurt this person as badly as I have been hurt. From a psychological point of view, this reaction lets off steam and may be "healthier" than complete repression of negative thoughts, but in the long run, it simply adds to the feeling of guilt I get for not being willing to forgive enemies more promptly.

A bit calmer, my next stage is to think about complete "sour grapes" withdrawal, not only from the immediate scene of struggle, but from all possible future confrontations. Since I love the rosary and also love my parish church, this fantasy takes the form of picturing myself having quit the active life, spending the entire day as a beadswoman praying the rosary and drifting into blissful contemplation. (I hope you are laughing not only at me but also at yourselves by now!)

But, since I am sure that God has not yet called me to the contemplative life, this phase only lasts about an hour, after which I begin to enter into the mystery of humility Saint Peter suggests in the passage above. I start meditating on the rejection Christ experienced, not only during the Via Dolorosa, but throughout his life on earth. I marvel that he, who could dwell in the perfect bliss of heaven with the Father, chose to come down into our life with all its pain, a sacrifice infinitely greater for him because he was not as blunt as we are. I remember that, as a Marian Woman in Ministry, like Mary, I am to identify with the Cross and be willing to be a burnt offering for the sake of the kingdom. I think that if Jesus looked at me mournfully and gave me a choice of being delivered instantly of all future sufferings or of suffering with him and for him in sacrifice for our battered Church of today, I would surely hope I had the grace to choose the Cross.

Thus recentered in my Savior, I begin to ask myself how I might respond positively to the setback involved in the particular rejection I have just experienced. I think about how good it would be not to give up but to try some new creative approach. Perhaps the Lord has something better in mind than the plan that didn't work. I count up the times when a rejection has led to something new in my life. Usually it is not long before some fresh idea for ministry presents itself, often simply by responding to some need of another.

Then, I turn to the consideration of my enemy. I ask

God in prayer if there is need for healing within me of some image of this person which comes from my own insecurities. I start what I call "digging an underground tunnel" into the soul of my opponent by praying for this person more often. I find it a great help in this stage to try to think about what life might be like for my "enemy". I pretend I am a writer concocting a short story about the average day of this person, trying to get the exact flavor of the staleness, discouragement, woundedness, confusion, and so forth, that might be tormenting him. In the process, I have come to realize that this is, in fact, one of the major vocations of fiction writers—to depict characters we normally dislike in a way that calls forth a merciful viewpoint. Very often Christ rewards this inner work of forgiving healing with a new and quite accurate image of the one who rejected me. In several quite dramatic cases, I have subsequently been able truly to love someone who I would heartily hate had I remained at one of my earlier stages.

Often I go to confession, contrite for the original caricature I had drawn of my enemy, especially in cases where I enjoyed transmitting this negative judgment to everyone I could find who might sympathize with me.

I realize that my delineation of these stages will seem quite extreme to those of you with blessedly milder temperaments. I have decided that God allowed me to have every fault so that his grace would be magnified as he heals me of them, slowly, oh, too slowly, meanwhile giving me the tongue and pen to describe boldly what others experience in a lesser manner.

A delightful joke touches on this struggle: "Don't worry. If you have succeeded in forgiving your enemies,

tomorrow will bring you some more." So, let us pray
for one another that we may overcome rejection by love
"forgiving them, for they know not what they do".

These reflections come from a leaflet by a writer-friend
in the single state:

"SOMETIMES I FEEL SO ALONE AND FORGOTTEN.

I Wonder Why God Created My Life?"

by Jeanne Berg

Many Catholics of good and sincere faith go through times
when they feel terribly lonely, as if forgotten by God himself.
Those who are single, widowed, or divorced may feel left out
of the love provided by marriage and family. Others who are
married or belong to religious communities also experience
periods of emptiness and loneliness for a variety of reasons.

I would like to discuss some of these questions and problems
that come up when people feel deserted and alone.

Could God really forget me?

This may seem like a ridiculous question at first, since we
know by the gift of faith and the teaching of the Church that
God is all-powerful and divine. But the gift of our faith is not
meant to prevent us from looking at the questions we have
inside about God's personal love and plans for our lives.

During times of struggle, many feelings of hurt or doubt may trouble us, but it's often the case that these reactions are closed away in our minds because of the fear that God would be displeased with feelings of anger or confusion.

God actually uses all our feelings, joyful or painful, to teach us more about ourselves and our needs. He wants us to feel free to recognize all our feelings so that he can then show us ways of growing beyond our hurts. Jesus himself felt the complete set of human emotions. He rejoiced to be with his friends and to see the wisdom of God's plan in the world. He was angry at injustice and disrespect of God's temple. He wept when he encountered death. He felt frightened and deserted at times during his Passion. He shared all his feelings with the people near him, with us, and with God the Father.

When the feeling of being forgotten or deserted comes, try simply telling God about it in your own words. Tell him the things that are on your mind. With a close friend, we can share fears or hurts and feel a great sense of relief afterward. God wants to be that kind of friend. Even if anger or despair is aimed at God himself, it can still be offered to God as a prayer because his tenderness can accept all our disappointments and confusion. Turning to him is like opening up a door; his deep, personal, and unconditional love can then enter and begin to heal.

God could not ever really forget you because you are like a part of himself, formed and created in his special love for you. The book of Isaiah in the Old Testament speaks of this love of God for you and each of us:

> Can a mother forget her infant, be without tenderness for the child of her womb? Even should she forget, I will never forget you. See, upon the palms of my hands I have written your name (Is 49:15–16).

*I feel like I don't belong anywhere,
I need more support from others.*

When you feel that other people do not know or care about you, try to practice seeing yourself as "part" of everyone you see rather than "separate". God's family takes in every human being, so everyone in the crowds we pass each day is actually a brother or sister whom the Lord knows extremely well, with longings and feelings much like those of all other people. One day we will all be completely familiar with each other, and the reaching-out for that joy can begin right now in the way we think about and treat each other.

Jesus referred to God the Father as "Abba", an affectionate term similar to our "Daddy". When we have no relatives or friends close by, it's good to remember that the closest and first community of love in my life is formed with God and myself. He wants to be close and familiar as "Abba". Even God himself shares life with the three divine persons of Father, Son, and Holy Spirit in one union. Once I remember that Abba is really always with me and thinking about me, it's easier to reach out to others.

Sometimes we think that telling others of our worries or loneliness would be a sign of weakness or perhaps inconsiderate. But often other people are touched by the trust you show when you tell them how you feel and are eager to let you know that they have often felt the same way too. So the act of sharing creates a bridge between two persons, with each one being enriched and feeling needed by the other.

If loneliness makes you feel that you are not really needed or important, discouragement sets in. But think about this image: a farmer has a large field, green with crops that are watered by an irrigation canal. A complicated system of sprinklers and timing devices keeps the water flowing. Another farmer also has a great crop in his field, but he doesn't use any irrigation system at all. Underneath his land is a hidden spring that brings water and coolness to the whole area. At times when you question the usefulness of your life, remember that God sees you as the mysterious hidden spring in his fields bringing life to many growing things through trust and hope.

MARGARET OF CASTELLO, O.P.

It was June 9, 1558. The coffin was carefully opened, leaving
the official witnesses awe-stricken. The clothing had crumbled
to dust, but the body was perfectly preserved. It was immediately evident to all that she had been a dwarf, her body
measuring only four feet long. Her head was rather large, out
of proportion with the rest of her thin body. The forehead was
broad, with the face tapering to the chin; her nose, quite
prominent; her teeth, small, even serrated at the edges. The
hands and feet were small. The right leg measured an inch and
a half shorter than the left, which caused her to walk with a
limp. The arms were crossed in front of the body, with the left
arm and hand being slightly raised without support. Following

Blessed Margaret of Castello (1287–1320) is a saint for the rejected,
lonely, or unwanted. Her story comes from the Blessed Margaret
Crusade.

a thorough and rigorous examination by a team of physicians, the body was reclothed in the Dominican habit and placed in a new coffin.

The birth of a deformed child is a traumatic experience for most parents. After the initial shock, grace and compassion conquer outright rejection. This was not so with Margaret's parents. Blessed Margaret of Castello was born dreadfully deformed. She was a dwarf, totally blind, hunch-backed and so lame she could hardly walk. Her father immediately ordered the child to be kept out of sight.

Afraid that the child would be seen if she remained in the castle, her father built a small cell next to the parish church in the forest. He thrust the unfortunate child into the cell and ordered the mason to wall up the doorway. Margaret was only six years old.

When she was seventeen, her parents took her on pilgrimage to Citta-di-Castello to the tomb of the saintly Franciscan friar, Giacomo, who—they hoped—would miraculously cure her. When that tactic failed, the heartless parents abandoned her.

Left to herself, Margaret was befriended by beggars, only to become one herself. Not long afterward, she joined the Mantellate, the first unmarried woman to become a Dominican Tertiary. Thereafter, several well-to-do families in turn gave her a home. Wherever she went, she brought peace.

Margaret was remarkable for clarity of mind and for infused contemplation. She willingly embraced her cross because she saw suffering through the eyes of faith. She did not know why God permitted her to have so many afflictions; but what she did know, was that he never permits one single misfortune without good reason. Margaret often wondered why people pitied her since she viewed her suffering as the expression of Christ's love for her and her means to gain heaven.

Pain made Margaret compassionate, sensitive, and understanding toward others. She visited prisoners, helped the sick, comforted the dying.

In spite of her handicap, Margaret was always joyful and courageous. She never became bitter, never complained, never reproached others, never lost heart. Rather, Margaret sought and found her strength in prayer and the sacraments. In every adversity, she turned to Jesus, Mary, Joseph and Dominic . . . there to find the courage to go on. And Margaret did go on . . . to achieve an intimacy with the Lord known only by those who love him uncompromisingly.

The body of Blessed Margaret, which has never been embalmed, now lies under the high altar of the Church of San Domenico at Citta-di-Castello, Italy. The arms of the body are still flexible; the eyelashes are present; the nails are in place on the hands and feet. The coloring of the body has darkened slightly, and the skin is dry and somewhat hardened; but by all standards, the preservation can be considered a remarkable condition, having endured for over six hundred and fifty years.

Had she been conceived today, Margaret surely would have been a victim of abortion or left to die at birth, and what a tragedy that would have been! A tragedy for Margaret who would have been deprived of the opportunity to suffer for Christ and thereby achieve the heights of sanctity; a tragedy for the Church who would have been deprived of such an extraordinary daughter; for each of us who, handicapped as we are by prejudice, by greed, by indifference, by cold-heartedness, or by whatever form it may take, would have been deprived of one with whom we can identify . . . of one who could truly show us that the only deformity abhorrent to God is the deformity of sin.

As an unwanted deformed child would she not be "the saint" for our time . . . a special patron of the unborn, the handicapped, the disabled, the social outcasts . . . the patron of the *unwanted*?

Here are some poems about loneliness—if reading them is painful, offer a prayer from the depths of the heart for yourself in your loneliness and for others who are far more lonely not knowing Christ as an interior friend.

Married Lady

Married Lady, how I envy you your cross.
You look at me and think
  She's thin, fashionably dressed
    I'd be that way . . . if it wasn't for my husband
      and children.
Do you know what it's like not to be touched!
I pray that your cross be not so heavy.
Please pray for me.

Kathy Hall

On Sorrow

Self-pity,
melancholy,
tragedy,
laceration—
No more!
An angel's wing brushed my soul.
Debris stings my eyes,
watered by longing
for the hidden homeland!

Ronda Chervin

One of the gifts to the Church that has come out of the charismatic renewal is the Healing of Memories, the emotional healing of life's wounds through encountering Christ's love in the midst of them. Here is a very simple prayer for healing:

A Prayer for Healing

You have shown me love and mercy all my life, Lord Jesus, I praise you! When I consider the love with which you suffered and died for me and the radiant joy with which you rose from the dead, I am filled with the desire to praise and thank you continually.

Yet, Lord, I dare to ask you for even more! We know, you and I, that I am wounded. In my own sins and the sins of others the reality of evil has touched me. Lord, heal me of these wounds. With your grace I renounce completely all attachment to my resentments against myself and others. I forgive with my whole heart anyone and everyone who has ever hurt me in any way and I pray sincerely to you for them.

Jesus, I join myself to that tremendous act of forgiveness with which you died and I love all those people who have come into my life. I embrace them with the very same love and tenderness which you have for them. I hold them up before you, Lord, that you may bless them and be kind to them. Give me your love, a love which destroys all resentments of my life. Heal me, Lord! I love you, I want to love you ever more and more. Thanks and praise be to your name forever and ever. Amen.

The Sorrows of Marriage

There are so many ways that women suffer in marriage and in all of these the love of Christ is crucial if we are to avoid sinking into the quicksand of despair.

For some it is a sense of being no longer loved as much as during the courtship period. For others there is disappointment that the spouse is not the man he appeared to be. Immoral choices and patterns plague some marriages in the form of infidelity, battering (psychological as well as physical), alcoholism, incest. Lack of communication on deeper emotional and spiritual levels can make a relationship become perfunctory and dissatisfying. Rivalry creates constant conflict in some marriages.

My own experience indicates three basic ways of meeting such heart-rending problems. Often together these ways can help and one alone is not sufficient.

1. The first approach is to develop a love-life with Christ so strong and so inclusive of every moment of daily life that Christ becomes the true spouse, not to the exclusion of the human husband, but so that the pressure is taken off of the fallible partner to fulfill needs that he could never fill perfectly in any case. If you love the Lord but have not attained a steady tangible relationship to him in prayer and the sacraments, the section on prayer in this book may be helpful.[1] Ask the Holy Spirit to guide you in trying new ways to let Christ's love come

[1] See pp. 189ff.

more completely into your heart. Women I know who have approached marital problems by turning to Jesus in this way notice that they become less desperate, nagging, sarcastic, bitter, and begin to love their husbands with a certain tender humor instead of seeing them as fallen idols. The change can be described in terms of the fairy tale about the princess and the frog. Before you fell in love with your husband to be, he seemed just like any other male frog in the pond. Falling in love changed him from a frog into a prince. Then it seems during marital distress that the prince went back to being a frog again. Developing a more resplendent love of Christ as the prince can make us more content to see ourselves as funny frog-couples—a bit like Kermit and Piggy—cute and silly, yet one day destined to fulfill our secret royal nature through grace.

2. A second complementary approach is to think through problems instead of adopting a passive outward attitude combined with interior anger or depression. Many women escape into fantasies in order to deal with pain and give up on any attempt to meet problems head-on. I wish, I wish, I wish replaces I will try this and this and this. Assertiveness in small ways can often make a big difference. For example, a woman whose domineering husband resents any time she might want to spend on her own activities may need to insist on a legitimate balanced number of such outside activities and just trust the Lord that he will help her husband to accept it.

3. Different forms of psychological or spiritual counseling, professional or informal, seem to be essential for many women. There can be false pride in not being willing to admit that we need help from others. God

may wish to use those he has inspired to develop their counseling gifts to help us. Being helped builds community. A friend of mine often says community is not built of all the strengths, but out of the need for each other that comes from weakness. What a warm feeling of gratitude I have for the many women and men who have helped me with my problems. In every case I would afterward wonder why I was so reluctant to seek their aid even when I was near to desperation. This advice is especially important when it comes to severe stress caused by problems such as alcoholism, infidelity, and battering.

Along with these approaches to marital unhappiness, there is always need for forgiveness. "The just man falls seven times a day." Fran Maier, editor of the *National Catholic Register*, once wrote that if we look closely we will see that forgiveness is our only source of joy in this life. Without forgiveness how would we ourselves be saved by Christ? Without forgiveness, how could we stand the company of anyone, even ourselves, for more than an hour?

The Sorrows of Mothering

The following are reflections about some of the sufferings of motherhood from my journal:

March 23, 1985

My Lord,
Yesterday was the twenty-second birthday of my twin daughters. We celebrated it today and in prayer with my

prayer-partner I was told to think of one of them as a little chick who will be reborn at Easter and the other as needing just to be held like a baby.

You know how some things in their lives at this time grieve me. They are so unhappy, yet still very loving and tender.

During the day one of them allowed me to pray over her if it also meant stroking her. She even agreed to giving the response to the rosary if I would only hold her and move my hand through her hair. She seemed exactly like the prophesied little baby who needs just to be held and cuddled.

When they were babies I used to call them squiggle-pusses. They are still very squiggly even though grown women.

Now I come to you, you who love them infinitely, and ask what I can do to bring them to you.

You reply that you do honor the penances I do for them and my humble prayers for their salvation. You want me to trust in you and also to trust in the good that I put into them through your grace all the years when they lived at home. You want me to show them that I see all the good in them which even their wanderings have not obliterated.

Thank you Lord for my children. Help young women to see how wonderful it is to be part of the creation of a new infinitely valuable human person. The older I get the more I appreciate my family. I want so much to be able to show that no matter what the crosses, what the burdens, it is all worth it.

To feel so much, means to suffer. A very loving mother of my acquaintance, who has older children whose ways are not her own, says that we must put our children into the chalice each Mass and offer them to Christ and then not take them back worryingly, but leave them in his embrace.

Here are two poems I wrote for my daughters which I am sure will find echoes in other mothers' hearts:

Diana

White lily floating down the jungle stream,
petals wide open to sun
and just as well to everyone!

Don't you fear
to be devoured by beasts?

You smile,
open your petals wider
on their green shiny pads
and drift out toward the sea.

Carla

Beauteous feline
scratching out the eyes of God
and ours, too—

Yet picking up
half-dead mice
in tender paws
warming them back to life!

Handicapped children

A different kind of suffering of mothers comes when a baby is handicapped severely—for, as handicapped activists rightly point out, everyone is handicapped in some way, but physical ones are more visible.

I asked a friend, Marie Engh, to describe her experience with her physically handicapped son. Here is her description:

Our sixth child was born in August, 1958. He was three weeks early and, though the birth was not difficult, I suspected something, what I was not sure. The next day, as I held him, his little body lacked strength; he felt like a little rag doll. The nurses were very kind and assured me all would be fine, but once or twice when the other mothers had their babies brought to them our little one didn't arrive. I was to find out later that the doctors were examining him to determine his problem.

In those days, you stayed in the hospital five days, and on the third day my husband arrived at visiting hours with tears in his eyes. He could barely get the words out of his mouth to tell me our child was a Mongoloid, a child with Down's Syndrome. My suspicions were not unfounded, but I surely did not expect this.

Neither of us knew what we were facing; we had no experience even knowing anyone with a child like this. At that time it was generally accepted that these children were placed in state institutions and rarely lived at home. It was the doctor's opinion that we should not take him home, but simply place him in the institution from the hospital. My husband had already spoken to a priest who concurred, as he felt it would be too difficult to care for the baby and the other five children, the oldest being only eight years of age.

The Sister at the Queen of Angels Hospital was of another opinion and encouraged us to bring him home, though she was careful to point out that it would not be an easy task. After hearing both sides, we were in such a state of shock and confusion that we asked permission to have him baptized and left in the hospital for a few days so that we might go home and have a little time to sort things out. In her kindness, Sister agreed to do this and we went home overwhelmed with sadness.

Those first few days were so difficult, and I remember waking up in the morning and wondering what terrible thing had happened to us, only to realize in a few moments what indeed was true. We looked into all aspects of placing our little son and as each hour and day passed, I felt sure the Lord was telling us we must at least try to care for him at home, no matter what the doctor said. Though my husband was afraid of the burden it might be, he agreed.

Our trip to the hospital was filled with apprehension, but the same Sister greeted us, and we left the hospital encouraged by her. I know she must have prayed for us as we do for her now.

We came home and began the slow process of adjusting to a totally unexpected situation. Those first months required so much time and patience with him, and patience with ourselves. Our children were loving and gentle with him and our relatives and friends were kind and helpful.

Our little one was placid and his development was very slow. Our expectations were minimal as the doctor had stated he might never sit, stand, walk or speak. When he took his first steps at twenty-six months and said his first words at age four it was cause of great celebration and thanksgiving. Each new development was a source of joy. Along with this, however, was a constant battle with strep throats, fevers, and so forth. He was hospitalized with severe flu when he was four, had a tonsillectomy at five, and open heart surgery at age six. The recovery from the heart surgery was traumatic and took several months, but it has improved his health greatly.

When our son was four years old we enrolled him in a day-care nursery school for the retarded and were fortunate to have a city public school open when he was eight. He learned to ride a bus each day to and from school. We were most grateful for the school and the years there were so rewarding. He is now employed at a sheltered workshop for the handicapped on a regular five day work week schedule. His capability of doing small tasks affords him the joy of being "grown up" and bringing home a real paycheck (the amount is of no consequence, it's the check that matters!).

An added blessing was a CCD class for the retarded which was held each Saturday in a neighboring parish. A wonderful devoted mother of a handicapped child taught the class. An equally devoted and compassionate pastor scheduled a special Mass one Saturday and our little boy received his First Holy Communion.

Through all these years our children have watched over him intently, helped teach him to walk, to talk, to print his name, to dance and even ride a bike. As parents we could not have asked for more compassion, concern, and support than they have given us. We have often reflected on how different our lives would have been if we had placed him in an institution. Who would have taught us patience (or tested it), who would have curbed our pride, taught us tolerance or helped us see the humorous side of things? We continue to learn each day things we could not have learned any other way.

Though we are often painfully aware of his developmental limitations, it has been of great interest to us to observe how he so often brings out the best in people he meets: the waitress, the clerk, the young teenager, a passerby who gives him a smile, a handshake, a kind word. Robert Christopher (Christbearer) in his simple way has been the disseminator of Christ's goodness and love. Though there are times of sorrow, he is a joy to us.

We thank the Lord for Robert and ask for the grace to

continue to care for him. Saint Paul writes: "We know that affliction makes for endurance, and endurance for tested virtue, and tested virtue for hope. And this hope will not leave us disappointed because the love of God has been poured out in our hearts through the Holy Spirit who has been given to us" (Rom 5:3–5).

Robert is a parishioner of my parish and I can attest that his parents are among the most admired people there for their courage, joyful patience, and radiant lives.

Miscarriage, stillbirth, abortion

Having had six miscarriages and knowing several couples who have had stillborn babies, I know how readily it is decided to push away the memory of such an occurrence. For this reason I was surprised and impressed by the ideas in a book called *Healing Life's Greatest Hurt* by Matthew Linn, Dennis Linn, and Sheila Fabricant concerning the need to pray for miscarried and stillborn babies. It is suggested that we name these children and make them part of the family by asking for their intercession. Repressing the memory can be very sad not only for the parents but also for other siblings who may grieve much more over these deaths than they reveal to us.

Abortion is one of the greatest sorrows of our world today. Heaven and earth weep over these senseless killings. It especially grieves those of us who are mothers to know that other women authorize the killing of their babies in utero because the baby will be poor, handicapped, the wrong sex, an embarrassment to them, or simply an inconvenience. And many childless couples who have not been so blessed with a pregnancy long to adopt such children.

Eileen Dennen suggests asking every woman who reads this to have a Mass said in her parish once, and more often if possible, in reparation for the sin of abortion. Here is a prayer she suggests to go in the bulletin the week of the Mass or more often:

> O Mary, Virgin Mother of the Holy Child, and Saint Joseph, you who protected them both, plead the endangered babies' cause in heaven for us. And help us always to "choose life" and never abortion. Hear us O Lord. Lord, hear our prayer.

Bishop Fulton J. Sheen has written another prayer begging protection of babies in danger of abortion:

> Jesus, Mary, and Joseph, I love you very much. I beg you to spare the life of the unborn child that I have spiritually adopted who is in danger of abortion.

My friends from Shield of Roses, a group that prays the rosary in front of abortion clinics and offers women alternatives, strongly suggest praying equally for the parents and for the abortionists as well. It is important also, as recommended by such groups as Catholics United for Life, that prayers be offered by repentant parents for their aborted child, naming the baby, and promising to make some kind of reparation. Of course, sacramental confession is essential. Hiding the sin can lead to serious mental and spiritual sufferings sometimes masked as depression which can lead to suicidal urges and acts.

Mary, Mother of unborn children, protect them.

The Sorrows of Working Mothers

Some years ago, I wrote a pamphlet entitled "The Working Mother: To Be or Not to Be" offering ideas about how to discern whether working outside the home is in the best interests of the family and really God's will.

There are some women who have no choice. It is a source of tremendous pain to have to leave little children all day in the care of others. There is a real need for adequate compensation for women who want to stay at home to take care of their children so that they will not be forced to leave them. Our Holy Father has often recommended some sort of system of a family wage or of other payments for parents.

In other cases both parents work in order to achieve a desired standard of living. More and more Christian women, however, are deciding that it would be better to live much more simply in order to be with their young children most of the day. Part-time work is often the ideal in such situations, or work that can be done at home.

Some women work outside the home because they have talents which are not adequately used in the home environment. Here, again, part-time is preferable, because the load of trying to work full-time and care for the home is terrible. The following is a prayer written by a Marian Woman in Ministry, Judy Esway, from the booklet "Prayers for Working Mothers":

Measure by Love

God, help me, a working mother, to measure each day by love. I set goals and try to follow a plan for keeping up with the house and laundry and my own personal interests; but now, three days have gone by. I've gone to the office, come home, had to run here and there; and nothing has been accomplished at home.

But as I was beginning to lament all of this, God, you touched me and told me to measure my day by love. You reminded me that love is the only measure of accomplishment. I remembered the meetings that took me away from home each night: parent-teacher conference, church meeting, my husband's office party.

It was love that made me close my eyes to "my plan" for the day. Help me, God, to always be open to "your plan" for my day. And remind me always to measure by love.

The Sorrows of Middle Age

Here are excerpts from a new book (not yet published) by Marian Woman in Ministry author Lois Donahue dealing with the problems of middle-aged women who find themselves "sandwiched" between the young and the elderly. With *wry* humor, Lois describes the particular sufferings of this age group:

THE SANDWICH GENERATION ON WRY

Being part of the "sandwich generation" certainly carries with it the very strong probability that we will feel the uncomfortable squeeze of being pressured between slices of the generation which raised us and the one which we are raising. To complicate things even further, here in the middle, we again face what we faced as a child, as a teenager, as a young adult and will face once more as a senior citizen—*the unknown*—and, as usual, it can be frightening.

We've never traveled these in-between miles before, and we are running into some brand new "firsts". First time Dad has a heart attack or Mom has a stroke. First exposure to nursing homes with their often depressing atmosphere and always exorbitant price tags. First indication that our own marriage or the marriages of our children might not truly be a " 'til death do us part" arrangement. First heartbreaking awareness that impersonal news stories can become very personal realities —drug addiction, unwanted pregnancies, homosexuality, physical abuse, suicide. For the first time we discover that we can no longer heal the hurts of our children simply with a hug, a cookie, or a bandaid, that grown children and extended family often take us out of the driver's seat, and that we are not the skilled doctor with all the cures or the wise counselor with all the answers.

Although most of us have built our own guard rail faith that keeps us from plunging into deep canyons of despair under such stress, still, frequent exposure to hills and curves and brick walls and traffic jams can make the going tough.

Unfortunately, too, we so often find ourselves alone. Not that we don't have friends and relatives who are stumbling along at our side, or the support and understanding of those trudging on parallel roads, or even the encouragement of those up ahead. Nevertheless, in the darkness of night, in the isolation of circumstances, and in the emptiness of time, there are those devastatingly lonely moments.

To complicate things even further, we seem to be forever skidding on guilt. Personally, I remember feeling guilty because I didn't wash, save, and reuse aluminum foil as my mother had done and then somehow feeling equally guilty because my daughter used twelve paper towels to wipe up a teaspoon of spilled milk. I felt guilty because I had varicose veins and bunions. I felt guilty because my children didn't go to Mass and my grandchildren didn't know the Act of Contrition.

But wait! I don't want to give the impression that life in the middle is a kind of obstacle course filled with nothing but foggy firsts and lonely, uncharted roads. That's not true. There are so very many God-smiling, cloud-free skies. There are safe, scenic roads, and their are "firsts" as warm and as pleasant as sunshine. Firsts like proud graduations and happy weddings and precious new babies. If one is lucky, there might even be a first financial breather somewhere along the way. Also, there may well be patches of time for oneself. To some there may be the almost euphoric quiet of the empty nest. For a great many there is the exhilaration of knowing that "left behind" are drag-along diaper bags, packed lunches, orthodontist visits, and car pooling.

In fact, it was during these middle years that I experienced what I know will be the most significant and rewarding "first" of my entire life. It was here that I first caught sight of my own spirituality—my own very personal relationship with God.

I don't even know exactly how, when, or why it happened. I was still the same old me—impatient with the clutsy driver in front of me, too easily distracted at Mass, operating my mouth before engaging my brain, breaking my Lenten promises. And God certainly didn't choose to introduce himself dramatically by knocking me to the ground or sending an off-duty angel. Instead it was almost as casual as a side-by-side "hi" over a sink of dirty dishes after the parish spaghetti dinner. That's it, I think, I met God *informally*. Oh, there remained the acknowledgment of his divinity, but I began to realize that I no longer always needed to kneel, head-bowed before a throne. Rather, I felt I could sit and talk with him under a tree beside the river Jordan if my imagination was in working order or, if not, at a kitchen table cluttered with dirty breakfast dishes. The spirit of my faith took shape, became real, and from then on I had the comforting certainty that never again would I be alone.

In a way, the part about never again being alone is almost amusing because God definitely did not arrive unattended. I soon found that he brought along his mother, his foster-father, his apostles (in fact the whole Bible branch of the family), his angels and his saints. Just as God seemed to step from prayer to become a person so, too, Moses and Miriam, Teresa and Catherine, Francis and Ignatius, Michael and Gabriel stepped from pages to become people, people who became family. (After all, a common Father makes for family ties be they of blood or baptism.)

I came to feel as rooted in spiritual ancestry to Abraham and Sarah from the Land of Canaan as to any Mike and Kate from the Emerald Isle. It was like being introduced to folks I hadn't even known were family. It was nice and homey and secure, *but* it did not lift me out of the reality of living. I still had to function and cope as part of the sandwich generation. I still felt the anguish of having a father and a daughter dying at the same time. I spent nights in worried prayer for a daughter dating an older, twice married man. During those same sleepless nights I knew anxiety for an aging aunt who might again don her robe and slippers and step into the darkness to walk "home"—a home which was merely a memory and some forty years and 2000 miles away. Somehow, though, it became different.

Probably because I gradually acquired the reassurance that whenever life shaped a cross for me to carry, regardless of its size or shape, somewhere in my spiritually extended family I could find a Simon of Cyrene to help make the burden lighter or a Veronica to show compassion.

The word "gradual" is important because there were definitely no instant miracles. (Instant is only for things like potatoes and puddings.) The fog didn't lift. The brick walls didn't crumble. The road didn't straighten nor the traffic jams magically disappear. Although, I must admit, I did learn two things rather quickly. One: I learned that at age forty I had not reached the "peak" from which leads the inevitable downward incline toward plot and headstone (the gruesome and depressing fate promised me by advertisers, designers and TV script writers). Two: I learned that forty was no more than another turn in the road, that free choice paths still stretched before me, and that life basically remained the same. I would chart the course and life would provide road blocks, pot holes, detours, and lousy weather conditions.

What I did learn little by little was that my spirituality was not something apart from my humanity. It wasn't something I could leave in the church pew, lock up between pages of written words or turn off with each Amen. It was there when I goofed and when I triumphed. It was part of my laughter and part of my tears. I was definitely a package deal—a permanent blend, body and soul, homogenized to the end. The trouble was, though, that for nearly half my life I had been primarily body conscious. I had never given my soul anything even close to equal time. Gradually I began to realize that it was the soul of me that had to grow, had to learn to smooth my life's edges, calm my life's storms, and clear my life's vision. Now I know that God gave me the mid-years to be that learning time for my soul. I know because it was somewhere between forty and sixty that I began to learn so many, many things.

The Sorrows of Widowhood, Separation, Divorce

None of my readers who are widows volunteered to share about their sufferings here. But I have spoken with quite a few widows and what comes forth shows how deep a wound this is for many women, even those whose marriages were far from perfect.

Most women agree on the stages of reacting to any death which have become so well known from the literature of psychology. Numbness is followed by anger at God, guilty feelings about unloving times, feelings of great sadness because there seems to be no way to make up for what was one's own fault in marital unhappiness, acute loneliness, and then eventually comes a time of making spiritual contact with the bereaved spouse and letting the happy memories flow in. One woman described to me an absolutely clear miraculous occurrence that God sent to help her realize that her husband was alive in eternity and still eager to help her out day by day. Many widows have so strong a sense of the spiritual presence of the beloved that they can talk to him by the hour.

An article in the Focolare Magazine by Mariele Quartana suggests prayers dedicated to Mary as a widow. It must have been hard for Mary to go from house to house, for she no longer would have a home of her own. Perhaps the Christian order of widows in the early times was designed to find a way that such women could use their gifts in ministry and would have a home in the Church as a spiritual mother to many others.

No separated or divorced woman came forth to speak

about their terrible suffering, although several promised to send them to me. I think that for many it is too painful to share.

When I think about this cross, my thoughts turn immediately to the marvelous woman saints who suffered in this way, such as Isabella of Spain or Cornelia Connelly.

The key to the heroic survival of faithful women who are separated or divorced seems to be in exchanging self-pity for forgiveness, self-absorbed brooding for outreach to others. One valiant woman who administers Catholic groups of divorced people claims that she readily prays for her husband and the woman he left her for without the slightest bitterness. Another woman's astounding love of Christ led her to witness about him to a whole string of women openly practicing adultery with her separated husband.

Hand Hold

For I have felt the clutching hand of fear
The clutching hand of fear
That here
   But here and now. But here and now
   The ending lay
And death would seal in nothing
Nothing
   Dear God that nothing-word has cancered
     in my heart
   Since when I found it eating out through
     frightened childish dreams

There was no place to run; no place to hide:
    no medicine; no comfort, none.
But all around me lay the wasteland, arid, empty,
    nothing.

  And then a calm
  Beneficent as balm
  With Easter sunrise, sorrow set.
God's grace a cloak of sarcenet,
Against the chill of fear wrapped comfort
    round my life.

And all my fears were lost
All my fears were lost in love
  In love, dear God,
  Dear God, of Thee.

                    Dr. Frank Sullivan

Healing Our
Feminine Faults

In 1985, in connection with the writing of *Feminine, Free and Faithful*, I began to study negative and positive feminine and masculine traits. I also began to give healing workshops on this subject.[1]

Here are some ideas about feminine traits which I encourage you to use to pray about your own personality. These are by no means exclusively feminine, but we can look at them in terms of our own feminine natures even if we do see them sometimes in men.

Check the traits on the list below which are your own. If not sure, ask yourself if others accuse you of them or if you have exhibited any of them at particularly important moments of your life:

angry	naive
weak	moody
passive	petty
slavish	prudish
wishy-washy	manipulative
seductive	nagging

[1] Workshop tapes can be obtained from Pecos Benedictine Monastery (see bibliography).

flirtatious
chattering
silly
sentimental

smothering
self-indulgent
extravagant

It might be good to go over this list with a relative or friend, for some negative traits you think are yours may have long since been overcome.

Now try to see what might be the root of the traits you have checked. For example, nagging might have come from a nagging mother. (If you haven't checked any, rejoice in the Lord and give thanks.)

These traits can be put into groups in terms of opposite virtues:

> Opposites to being *strong* are being weak, passive, slavish. An opposite to *gentleness* is anger. Some opposites to *purity* are seductiveness and flirtatiousness. Opposites to being *wise* are being silly, naive, sentimental, wishy-washy. Opposites of *self-control* are chattering, self-indulgence, extravagance, moodiness. It is un*trusting* to be petty, nagging, smothering and manipulative. Being *responsive* (according to your state in life) to God's creation in sexuality is an opposite to being prudish.

Going through Scripture with the assistance of a concordance is a way to find instances of the virtues which are opposite to your faults. Write out or make a note of your favorites to reflect on each day. Here are some examples:

> *strength:* 1 Kings 2:1–2; Psalm 24:8; Psalm 136:12; Proverbs 23:11; Proverbs 31:10–31; Isaiah 35:3–4; Luke 1:80; Romans 4:20; Ephesians 6:10–20; Judith 11, 15.

courage: Joshua 1:9; 1 Chronicles 19:13; Psalm 27; Lamentations 1:16; John 11:16; 2 Corinthians 6:3–10. Also, making the Stations of the Cross can give us courage as we realize how much Jesus suffered.

gentleness: Proverbs 15:4; Jeremiah 11:19; John 8 (Christ's gentleness to the woman taken in adultery); Matthew 5:22; Matthew 11:29; Galatians 5:22.

compassion: Deuteronomy 13:17; Psalm 145:9; Isaiah 40:1–2; Isaiah 54:8; Isaiah 66:12; Hosea 11; Luke 7:13; Luke 10:29ff.; Luke 15; Luke 23:34; Colossians 3:12.

self-control: Proverbs 25:28; 1 Corinthians 7:5; 1 Corinthians 9:25; Galatians 15:16–25; 2 Timothy 1:7; 2 Peter 1:6; Titus 1:8.

purity: Psalm 24:4; Psalm 51; Matthew 5:8; Matthew 5:28; Galatians 5:19; Romans 1:26; Jude 1:7; Titus 2:5, 12; 1 Peter 3:1–7.

tenderness: The Song of Songs.

Another approach to healing feminine faults is the Healing of Memories. It consists in going back into the past and inviting Christ into the moments of deprivation or pain that might have led to these negative traits. Here is a meditative prayer I wrote for this purpose:

Dear Lord,

We come before you, your women, with many wounds of the past. Perhaps a father, mother or parental figure did not want us to be born of the female sex because of disparaging the feminine in themselves or in society. And so, such a parent may have failed to bring out our feminine charm and playfulness so that we are now less than responsive.

But you, Lord, created us male and female with equality of

worth (Genesis). You formed us in our mother's womb. You wanted the unique soul of each woman to be clothed in feminine form.

Let us pause now and try to get an inkling of the delight you had when you conceived each of us as female or male. . . .

Some of us had mothers or fathers who felt distaste for their own bodies or for those of the opposite sex, and they transmitted these attitudes to us by their body language.

Some of us had parents or relatives who unconsciously or very actively felt lustful toward us as females. This may have made us self-conscious, fearful, or manipulative in our own way of living in our bodies.

But you, Lord, shaped our bodies as well as our souls, as a potter shapes the clay. Let us feel your reverent wonder in the way we are made.

Let the touch of your hands remove any memories of disgust or of guilt caused by our childish response to such disordered attitudes or acts of others, leaving their legacy of prudery or seductiveness or lust.

Many of us felt unattractive in our youth, our teens, or later, by comparison to the perfect images of woman in the media or because of our envy of more popular siblings, schoolmates, co-workers. We were too short, too tall, too fat, too thin.

But, Lord, You made us all shapes and sizes. You like variety, not paperdoll stereotypes. Help us to see that you like the way we look, funny little creatures that you made. You have counted every hair on our heads, you know each line, each wrinkle, each bump. You want us to laugh at ourselves more.

Some of us felt unappreciated by members of the household or institution we were reared in, made fun of or bullied by the kids at school or in the neighborhood. As a result we became closed or bitter, angry, and controlling. Yet you were there in our innermost depth cherishing us.

Let us experience your perfect love for us as individuals right now so that we may accept the cross of the past as a way of preparing us to give the affirmation to others we so sadly missed ourselves.

When we look further into our hearts we find other negative imprints of the past. Some of us as girls or as women were forced into the role of slaves to the men in the family. Our service was not free in the Spirit, and now we do not know how to give without resentment. Show us the compassion you felt for us when we were Cinderellas. Send your Mother to teach us how to give as a gift of love.

If our parents were domineering, nagging, or unpredictable, we may feel that we have to control ourselves and others in order to be safe. But you guide without force, gently inviting us to follow freely. Let us breathe deeply in the luxuriating space you give us. Help us to avoid smothering those we love. Let us reverence their individual paths, trusting in your providence.

Many of us as girls and women were taught that to gain love we had to succeed at countless little tasks to please others. We have fallen into patterns of compulsive exterior goodness without the freedom to flow with inner love. Open us in prayer to the interior freedom of wanting to do good from the Spirit's initiative, developing the gifts you have given us.

In our later life some of us have been victims of infidelity. This has left us feeling rejected, ugly, unlovable. Help us, Lord, to identify with you, the most rejected of all men, to forgive as you did, and to experience our attractiveness as one loved and wanted intensely by you.

In mid-life or old age we may feel our feminine charm disappearing. We may want so much to feel reassured in our femaleness that we are tempted to or actually do betray our commitments. We ask you, Lord, to send us true Christian friends who will affirm us and also to give us a clearer vision of our lovableness now and the supreme beauty of our bodies and souls as they will flourish in the eternal kingdom.

Teach us, Lord, to believe in Christian love, to value the movements of the heart more than status in the world. Lord, we cry out to you, make us, your women, as lushly feminine and free as your women saints, your brides. Let us know that you exalt over us.

> I will greatly rejoice in the Lord,
> my soul shall exult in my God;
>
> for he has clothed me with the garment of salvation,
> he has covered me with the robe of righteousness,
> as a bridegroom decks himself with a garland,
> and as a bride adorns herself with her jewels.
> For as the earth brings forth its shoots,
> and as a garden causes what is sown in it to spring up,
> so the Lord God will cause righteousness and praise
> to spring forth before all the nations.

> Isaiah 61:10–11

After using this prayer with a partner or in a group, you may want to have special prayers for areas which this healing exercise brought to mind.

From Passive or Aggressive to Firm and Humorous

Many women have a great deal of difficulty with assertiveness. We tend to be temperamentally passive or aggressive and it is a real struggle to come instead into patterns of firm assertiveness.

There is a good kind of passivity which can better be called receptivity. Jeanette Crosetti, a Marian Woman, writes, "I used to think of passivity as a negative description of behavior. Passivity would equate with lack of responsibility, complacency, a giving away of one's control. However, passiveness can be good. It can be good when we turn away from our ego desires and allow the Lord to activate his will in our lives! He tells us what he wants, we receive, we listen, we follow. As we follow, we grow more intimate, we grow closer to our Lord and Heavenly King."

There is another kind of passivity which is not good at all. Here is Saint Teresa of Avila's humorous description of this kind of fear:

> If your spirit begins to quail it will do great harm to what is good in you and may sometimes lead to scrupulosity, which is a hindrance to progress both in yourself and in others. It will not lead many souls to God if they see that she is so strict and timorous. Human nature is such that these characteristics will frighten and oppress it, and lead people to avoid the road you are taking. . . . Bear in mind that God does not pay great attention to all the trifling matters which occupy you, and do not allow these things to make your spirit quail and your courage fade.

Reading about women saints of great courage and trust in the Lord can inspire us to pray for greater courage in our own lives.

CATHERINE OF SIENA

The story of Saint Catherine of Siena (1347–1380) is good reading when you're up for something spectacular and dramatic and don't plan to sleep until the book is done. You wouldn't be able to put it down. *The Life of Saint Catherine of Siena* by Father Raymond of Capua, her confessor, or any other biographies or chapters telling her tale, will have you rapt with attention. If we were to compare Catherine to a phenomenon in nature, it might be a cracking bolt of lightning, so riveting an appearance did she make in her day. She had a fresh, magnetic way of illuminating things and waking people up.

Take Pope Gregory XI, for example. Catherine single-handedly persuaded him confidently to challenge the French king and the entire Sacred College and return to Rome— ending a *seventy-year* Babylonian Captivity of the popes in Avignon, France. Later the same Gregory authorized her to act as his delegate in dealing with the rulers of Florence. Heads of state and Papal legates tracked her down or sent messengers to fetch her so they could glean her input on political and Church concerns. When her native land was ravaged by civil wars and factions, she journeyed from one powerful noble to another attempting to heal those wounds. And in the last years of her life Catherine assumed agonizing sacrifices to sustain the Church during the Great Schism.

Few people realize that the mystical Catherine, black sheep among medieval women, refused to be wife or nun. Independent and mobile, she becomes an interesting model for single Catholic women approaching the twenty-first century. It was precisely in that state, untied to family or communal life, that she was free to take her mystical and miraculous gifts to the streets—to the poor, the sick, the searching, the rich, and the powerful. In many ways Catherine of Siena had the bite and fire of a modern feminist. But the source of her successful liberation was always Christ, her Master and true Love.

Another thing that many people don't realize about this ascetic contemplative saint is that she was raised in one of the noisier houses in fourteenth century Siena. She had not five, not ten, not fifteen, but *twenty-three* brothers and sisters. Catherine's prosperous father, Giacomo Benincasa, a wool-dyer, and her vivacious mother Lapa managed a sprawling house of two dozen boisterous children, sometimes including married couples and grandchildren. The image we construe of the Benincasa household is one of love and laughter, but also one of clutter, noise, and distraction. And yet this was the hothouse where God planted one of the Church's rarest mystics.

Jesus "courted" Catherine when she was just a child, clearly marking her for special gifts from all eternity. One evening when she was six, walking home in the streets of Siena after visiting a married sister, Catherine lost pace with her brother Stephen and stood transfixed. Stephen found her gazing rapturously in the sky above the roof of the Church of the Friars Preachers (the Dominicans). She was feasting her eyes on Christ the King, radiant in glory with his Apostles Peter, Paul, and John. The royal majesty of Christ was so enticing that little Catherine wanted to gaze at him forever. When her brother finally shook her from the vision, she burst into tears. "Oh if you but saw what I was looking at," she told him, "you would never have tried to take me away from a sight so delightful!"

A year later, when she was seven, Catherine precociously vowed to give her whole life to God. At this time she used to spend long hours by herself, thinking about God and praying to him.

Those formative years of contemplation were a cornerstone

for lifelong intimacy with Christ. But interludes of the mundane inevitably cropped up in the Benincasa clan. When Catherine reached twelve, her mother and sister started hinting that she do the little beauty rituals that would attract a man. She showed little interest—after all, she had already given her heart to Christ—but in time the persuasion wore her down. Once her sister Bonaventura talked her into painting her cheeks and bleaching her hair.

An incident happened shortly after that which snapped Catherine back to reality: Bonaventura died. As she witnessed the quick disruption of what was a vibrant, beautiful, earthly life—and considered that her sister was yesterday combing her hair and today in eternity—Catherine resolved never to acquiesce to her family's prodding again. In retrospect during the later years of her life, she always felt bitter disappointment for having "given into vanity" for that brief period, and she performed many penances in reparation.

When Catherine informed her family that she now wished to live like a hermit they were a little disgruntled. First, the refusal to marry like a normal fourteenth century maiden, now the audacity to retreat from family life. To make a point, Catherine cut off her long hair, cropping it as short as a boy's. This action, interpreted as defiance, made her family all the more determined to integrate her back into the Benincasa mainstream. They made her a servant from sunup to sundown doing menial chores. We picture Catherine, a wilful teenager, elbow deep in scrubbing water, determined to hold her ground.

But by all reports she did it so sweetly and patiently that no one could rattle her peace. Years later in *The Dialogue*, Catherine's written collection of her conversations with Christ, she revealed that God taught her how to build in her soul a secret cell where no tribulation could enter, a quiet refuge in the center of her heart. No matter how rigorous or distasteful the chores became, Catherine enjoyed ecstasy in that interior cell where she kept constant and delightful communion with our Lord.

Then one night in a dream she saw a group of the great founders of convent life. Saint Dominic impressed her most, and he also seemed fascinated with her. In the dream he approached her and held out a black and white garment and told her one day she would wear it. It was the dress of the Third Order Dominicans, the tertiaries known in Italy as the Mantellate. These people lived in their homes but assembled together for prayer in the chapel of San Domenico church.

When she awoke from that sleep, Catherine was as immovable as a chunk of granite. She begged her father to let her cloister herself in some quiet niche of the house. No more dishes, no more laundry, no more noise—just sweet communion with the Lord of her heart. In this sense Catherine of Siena was a type of Martha's sister Mary of Christ's day. She had discovered that "the better part" was to sit at his feet; and unlike Martha, she chose that better part.

Her father softened, and she was allotted a soundless room above the kitchen. Pilgrims to Siena today can still visit this room. They would find it small and stark, just as Catherine liked it. Her furnishings were a chest and a bench, the bench serving as a table by day and a bed by night. A log of wood was her pillow, and the only light she ever saw in the quarter was from a little candle lamp.

For the next three years Catherine was happily at home in that obscure dwelling. Mystical graces and visions and gifts came to her there. Temptations did too. One time she was frighteningly accosted by the devil and a horde of alluring figures. She panicked and tried to shut them out of her thoughts, but they kept persisting and taunting her. When her soul could take it no more, the horrible vision faded away and Christ came, bathing the cell in light. Catherine asked him where he could have been while she was so tormented, and he told her, "I was right in the middle of your heart." That story parallels the cases of so many other holy persons who try to please God—and it assures us that darkness can never encompass us when our soul is in grace.

Although Catherine's austerities ranked her with the great hermits, the Third Order Dominicans at first refused her—again, encouragement for those of us who seek a certain vocation or calling and at first find it surrounded with obstacles. The tertiaries refused her on the basis of youth and mystery. Youth because she was barely out of her pre-teens. Mystery because they had never met a girl of her kind. Eventually, learning that she performed the severest penances of them all—sleeping one half hour every two days, fasting on bread and vegetables—and finding her extremely mature and intelligent in conversation, they took her into their group. Thereafter, Catherine spent all her time in one of *two* places: her cell at home and the San Domenico church. She was sixteen years old.

Life as a recluse may sound dull to most of us, but Catherine found ecstasy in ways that only a handful of people do across the centuries of humanity. In this lifetime, on earth, she had a direct foretaste of heaven. Often Christ appeared to her, with his Mother or in the company of his friends the Apostles, Mary Magdalen, Saint Dominic. They enjoyed conversations and friendship, so in a very real sense this female hermit was never alone.

Perhaps they were keeping her social skills finely tuned, reminding her of the encouraging power of love. In time they would expect her to use it. But first, as a lasting sign of her three years in seclusion with him, Christ appeared to Catherine with a very special gift. It was Mardi Gras, or Shrove Tuesday, 1367. All the households of Siena were wining, dining, and making noise in the streets. Catherine alone was keeping him company. He came before her, took her hand, and gave her a gold and jewel-encrusted ring. He told her this:

I, your Creator and your Savior, wed you today and I
present you with a faith that will never falter and will be
preserved from all taint until the day of our wedding in
heaven. Fear nothing. Vested with the armor of faith, you
will triumph over all enemies.

Thereafter, Catherine was always able to see the ring, though
it was invisible to all around her. Without ever becoming a
nun, then, Catherine was a spouse of Christ.

Shortly thereafter Christ asked her a favor that was the last
thing on her mind. He asked her to go downstairs and have
dinner with her family. Naturally she obeyed him. Imagine
the shocked look on the faces at the Benincasa table, the relief
of her mother, the surprise of her father, and the curiosity of
her brothers and sisters. She returned to the sights and sounds
and smells of her family's ordinary life. And that proved to be
the threshold of Catherine's vocation in the rest of Siena and all
of Europe.

The only thing that can explain the tremendous leap she
took from obscurity to fame is God's grace and plan. Almost
immediately the artists, musicians, scholars, priests, laity,
and laborers of Siena found in her a spiritual mother. She
affectionately called this assortment of faithful personalities
her "bella brigata". She had the uncanny mystical gift of
reading hearts. When one of her disciples was giving in to a
temptation, she summoned him and the look in her eye
quickly changed his mind. She spoke of all the things that she
had learned during her three-year sabbatical from the bustle of
the world—she told them what Christ was like, what he
wanted men and women to know and do, and why it was so
important to keep one's eyes on eternity.

As her contacts increased, voluminous correspondence became a necessity. She had several male secretaries handle that
flow. Meanwhile, as she approached her twentieth birthday,

Catherine tried to learn to read herself. She was trying to manage the alphabet and making small progress when she asked our Lord to teach her. Overnight she was reading fluently the Gospels, Saint Paul's Epistles, and the Breviary. Eventually she also learned to write, explaining it to her spiritual director like this: "I took lessons, as if while sleeping, from the glorious evangelist Saint John and Saint Thomas Aquinas."

This infused scholarship was the bridge that carried her into the political and ecclesiastical spheres that she would influence and build up. Skill and self-assurance gave her the upper hand with everyone, from the most sophisticated and refined to the crustiest of old prelates. She was determined to make the world a better place.

She was also determined to ease each individual's sufferings as she found them. During the hideously contagious Black Plague that swept through Europe, Catherine became a heroine in her city. She picked up the victims with her own hands and cared for them as if each one were Christ himself. Much like our Mother Teresa of Calcutta, she was sensitive to the needs of the human soul for dignity and love in the darkest hours.

One of Catherine's most famous patients was a cantankerous leper named Tecca. Tecca was so pitiable that no one would come near her, let alone touch and love her. Catherine took it upon herself to cradle and bathe and shower tender care on Tecca—even though Tecca hated and insulted her. Catherine even contracted leprosy on her hands during this time, but she continued to treat Tecca like she would a beloved child or parent. Gradually Tecca's hard, frightened heart was gentled and she died believing Catherine was a saint.

Blessed Raymond of Capua, Saint Catherine's spiritual director and biographer, wrote of another striking case:

> On one occasion, when she [Catherine] happened to be so
> ill that her whole body was swollen up from head to foot

and she could not get out of bed or put a foot under her, she heard of a poor widow who lived in the district adjoining her own. This poor woman had a family of boys and girls, all of them suffering great hunger and want. Catherine's heart was moved with compassion, and when night came on she prayed her Lord to give her back for the time being strength enough to bring help to the poor woman. Before dawn broke, she got up and began to ransack the house. She got a sack and filled it with wheaten meal, a great glass bottle which she filled with wine, another bottle which she filled with oil, and such edibles as she could find, bringing them all to her little cell. But it was one thing to be able to bring these articles one by one to her cell and quite another to find the strength to carry them all together the whole way to the widow's house. It seemed impossible.

However, she took up the goods and fastened them about her weak body, one article on her right arm, another on her left, something on her shoulders, something else hanging from her waist. Then, placing her hope in the help of heaven, she made an effort to stand upright laden with her burden. Instantly, by God's wonderful help, she heaved it all up with such ease that it felt as if each of the things she carried had been drained completely of its weight. . . . And yet, according to a careful reckoning which I [Raymond] worked out myself, the goods which she was carrying at the time normally would have weighed about a hundred pounds.

Such stories run throughout Catherine's life, for her heart was a channel of God's great love. Her touch and her wisdom healed the bodies and souls of many women and men and whole jurisdictions in late medieval Italy.

"I want you to fly to heaven on *both* wings", Christ once told her in her little cell off her father and mother's kitchen.

He meant by interior, contemplative love for him and by out-going generous love for her neighbors. Nothing in Catherine's life ever let either wing get clipped. Great woman, great saint, and Doctor of the Church, she shows us the way to soar to those heights.

As you can see, Catherine of Siena is a wonderful example of holy assertiveness. She was not at all fearful of following God's special call to her and she would let no obstacle keep her from love of God or neighbor.

I do not tend toward fearful passivity either, but rather toward raging anger. This anger keeps me from positive assertiveness, because instead of quietly figuring out with the help of prayer how to overcome obstacles, I simply stew in the juice of my own resentments.

Here are some passages about anger that have helped me to bring annoyances to Christ and to seek peaceful solutions:

> There is no sin nor wrong that gives a man such a foretaste of hell in this life as anger and impatience.

> Catherine of Siena

Saint Paul says in Ephesians 5:29–32:

> Never let evil talk pass your lips; say only the good things men need to hear, things that will really help them. Do nothing to sadden the Holy Spirit with whom you were sealed against the day of redemption. Get rid of all bitterness, all passion and anger, harsh words, slander, and malice of every kind. In place of these, be kind to one another, compassionate, and mutually forgiving, just as God has forgiven you in Christ.

The same Paul also says in Galatians 5:22–23:

In contrast, the fruit of the Spirit is love, joy, peace, patient endurance, kindness, generosity, faith, mildness, and chastity.

Avoid disputes, make light of temporal crosses and forget injuries, otherwise you will not be really alone, even when you have no visible company.

Saint Bernard

Worry and trouble are for hell; the children of God ought not to know them.

Venerable Francis Liebermann

To err is human, to forgive divine.

Alexander Pope

It is not always necessary to argue, but it is always necessary to love.

Schwarz

The following three are my own reflections on anger:

I cross the rapids of resentment on the sturdy boat of forgiveness.

When I try to make myself the center of reality, everything is irksome, refusing to conform to my plan. When I see you as the center of reality, everything is interesting, a kaleidoscope image of your plan.

Lest the eye get too sharp, and the upper lip too stiff, God sends the gift of tears.

God's servants who have had the highest and most exalted inspirations have been the gentlest and most peaceable men in all the world. . . .

On the contrary, the evil spirit is turbulent, bitter, and restless. Those who follow his hellish suggestions in belief that they are heavenly inspirations can usually be recognized because they are unsettled, headstrong, haughty, and ready to undertake or meddle in affairs. Under the pretext of zeal they subvert everything, criticize everyone, rebuke everyone, and find fault with everything. They are men without self-control and without consideration who put up with nothing. In the name of zeal for God's honor they indulge in the passions of self-love.

Francis de Sales

One of the greatest helps I have found in overcoming anger caused by the give and take of dealing with opposite personalities comes from study of the Myers-Briggs Personality Test. It explains how, without the slightest malice on either side, people with different characters will find each other hard to live with. The main opposites tested for involve introversion and extroversion, sensory interests versus love of exploring intuitive possibilities, thinking and feeling, and orderly planning versus flexible play-it-by-ear styles of doing things.

For example, being much more extroverted, I find it hard to realize how much my husband cherishes solitude and how hard it is for him to endure day after day of social activities. It doesn't mean that he hates people, just that he gives better in small intense times than diffused over many friends over long periods. Loving to explore intuitive possibilities, I have had to realize that more sensate types get impatient with my daydreams. They want to know about what is real, right before their eyes. I have come to admire the way sensory people can enjoy the now and concentrate on intricate mechanical projects.

The fact that I like to plan every hour of my life years ahead makes me very frustrated with those who will not plan even a day in advance. But, working with this I can see how often it is easier to follow the Holy Spirit if a person is more flexible than I am.

In prayer it is worthwhile to consider the different temperaments of those close to us and to ask God for the grace not to become too irritable because everything isn't just as one would want it to be. It is also good to remember that a person's virtues are often linked to his chief sources of difficulty—many charming people are more unreliable than your dull plodding type; a spontaneous and generous person may often make mistakes for lack of thoughtful prudence.

A friend, Melinda Brogan, offers the following way of dealing with anger:

> Whether our anger is justified or not, anger is unhealthy in its impact on our bodies. Certainly if we are outraged by an injustice, anger is useful to incite us to act against evil. But all anger is only useful if it can be used constructively and not harbored within us. How many times when a loved one has wounded us we are filled with so many different emotions that we have no idea how we can ever regain control of ourselves and quiet the situation. We may make rash threats that we will never carry out and lose credibility for our side.
>
> There is a remedy. After you fill up with emotion and feel your insides quaking, get off by yourself with a pen or pencil and write just what you mean to say. Include

necessary apologies for those hurtful stabs you carelessly threw out when you lost contact with your reasonable nature. I strongly believe in writing letters to those who outrage us, because once we are in print and seem likable even to ourselves, we feel a sense of being in control. We can cut out all those fillers we throw into our arguments that only detract from our points. Also, we have tangible proof of what sorts of issues create this loss of control within us, and so, as these arise in the future, and they will, we can discover a lot about our insecurities and repetitive patterns. Writing brings order and meaning to otherwise regrettable outbursts.

Marian Woman Theodora Spero writes:

Oh! How I can relate to having negative thought patterns, and Oh! how I desire constantly to take every thought captive and make it obey Christ (2 Cor 10:5). I find this more easily done by submitting my emotions to the Holy Spirit to be brought under his control. Also, I find it extremely important to offer my tongue, mind, heart, and entire being for the greater honor and glory of Almighty God (Rom 12:1–2; Phil 4:6–8).

In particular I ask him to transform my heart into Mary's Immaculate Heart. Mary's intercession is required at all times as she moves so harmoniously with the Holy Spirit. Saint Louis Marie de Montfort's *True Devotion to Mary* teaches the beautiful way of placing all that we have into the hands of Mary (Rev 5:8).

Dana Black sent us a prayer of forgiveness written by a young Jewish boy in a Nazi concentration camp, found in a crumpled up paper scrap by his body. It makes one very ashamed of nurturing resentment:

O Lord, remember not only the men and women
   of goodwill
but also those of ill will.
But do not only remember the suffering they have
   inflicted on us,
remember the fruits we bought, thanks to this suffering,
our comradeship, our loyalty, our humility,
the courage, the generosity,
the greatness of heart which has grown out of all this.
And when they come to judgment
let all the fruits that we have borne be their forgiveness.

We have a wonderful model in Mary for cultivating
peace, for example, in her message at Fatima. Also, in
1946, our Lady was reported to have appeared in Marien-
fried, Germany. This was just after the war, and her
message concerned how to pray for peace in our own
hearts and to do penance to avoid future world wars. The
apparitions in Medjugorje, not yet officially approved,
convey the same message as those of Fatima. We should
never cease to pray to Mary for an end to destructive
anger and revenge.

From Temptation to
Joy in the Lord

Many women I know are plagued by temptations of a
sexual nature. It is comforting to find that saints and holy
people also had such problems and their thoughts about
it can give us wisdom:

No man is so perfect and holy as not to have sometimes temptations; and we cannot be wholly without them.

Thomas à Kempis

The devils enter uninvited when the house stands empty. For other kinds of guests, you have first to open the door.

Dag Hammarskjöld

For the law of sin is the fierce force of habit by which the mind is drawn and held even against its will, and yet deservedly because it had fallen wilfully into the habit.

Saint Augustine

> To what a cumbersome unwieldiness
> and burdensome corpulence my love had grown
> But that I did, to make it less
> And keep it in proportion,
> Give it a diet, made it feed upon
> That which love worst endures,
> *discretion*.

John Donne

The topic of temptation as it applies to serious sin has been mentioned earlier in this book. Most Christians know that one should absolutely avoid near occasions of sexual sin of whatever kind. It is no good to play with fire. Avoiding sin is very unlikely if we take chances by arranging romantic occasions.

But what about those of us who, while avoiding occasions of sin, nevertheless build up elaborate fantasies about alternate lives we might be living . . . if only!

I have not fully worked out a spirituality about fantasies, so I will only share with you reflections which from time to time I have found helpful in this area. I have the impression that women who fall into fantasy do so with even more vehemence than most men, possibly because we value intimacy so highly that when we are not getting along too well with our nearests and dearests we almost feel compelled to fill the void with images of perfect alternate relationships.

I find myself that times of intense fantasizing often coincide with times of lack of challenge in my life. If I am treading water in my spiritual and intellectual life, then the emptiness is readily filled with fantasies.

Most deeply I find that fantasies go along with lack of trust in God's providence. It is as if I would say to God, "I'm not all that sure that you will come through, maybe in heaven, but I have a long life before heaven, possibly, and I can't stand the humdrum nature of my daily existence a moment longer."

It is good to refresh my imagination with images of eternal happiness, union with all those I love, and especially union with my beautiful Savior Jesus Christ.

One needs to realize that sexual fantasies can become an enslavement to the devil, and that we must love instead the Body of Christ in the Eucharist and his people. I meditate on the fact that if someone wanted to enslave me in a concentration camp or Gulag, I would flee. So why do I give in so swiftly to the devil's suggestion that I waste my precious time on fantasies of sins I would never want to commit? "The violent bear it away." Pray with the same intensity you pour into fantasies and let Christ transform the violence of Eros into a furnace of love for him. Did not the saints flagellate themselves, throw themselves into thorn bushes, plead with God, and in that way use their temptations as doorways to the mystical experience of his love?

MARY MAGDALEN

Deep waters cannot quench love,
Nor floods sweep it away.

Song of Songs 8:7

One of the most consoling exposures of our Lord's character
involved a party and a woman. It took place in Bethany one
night at the home of Simon, a rich Pharisee well-connected
with the scholars, thinkers, and most respected men of his day.
Simon summoned all of the high Jewish community to his
house for a celebration banquet honoring a Guest that had
cured his leprosy. The Guest was Christ, healer and teacher
who was still an object of their speculation, but whose miracles
had stopped them in their tracks.

The intercession of Saint Mary Magdalen, the loving, repentant
woman of the Gospels, can help us to overcome temptation.

Into this private bash of self-righteous Pharisees walked a stunning woman. Even holy women of those days were barred from such affairs. But this woman was particularly out of place. She was Mary Magdalen, a village prostitute, a Jezebel, a seductress of the night, in ordinary parlance a hooker or a tramp. Her extraordinary entry stirred a collision of emotions in the men. All of them, some perhaps secretly and hypocritically attached to her, started to murmur against her.

But Mary had come with the kind of purpose Saint John lauded when he said that "perfect love casts out fear" (1 Jn 4:18). She walked straight to Jesus of Nazareth at his table, knelt before his tired, dirt-caked feet and pressed them to her lips. She started to weep, cleansing his feet with her tears and wiping them with her hair. Then she took out an alabaster box full of the most precious ointment money could buy and anointed his head and feet.

Saint Mark tells us that the ointment was spikenard, a rare and treasured balm worth three hundred silver pieces. He also wrote that Mary broke the alabaster box. She could not get it to flow quickly enough, so great was her urgency to pour everything she could give before the Lord.

Jesus shocked the Pharisees by regarding this most public and despised sinner with the tenderness of a loving father and friend. "Your sins, many though they be, are forgiven because you have loved much", he told her. Then he answered Simon's secret thoughts by telling the whole room the parable of a creditor who forgives two people in debt, one owing five hundred pence and the other fifty. "Who do you think loves the creditor more?" he asked. "The one who was forgiven more", they answered—and they had learned one more lesson about the kingdom of God.

It is important to remember that Mary Magdalen's sins were grave, deeply embedded, and very numerous. Scripture tells us that she had to be released from seven demons. Her lifestyle produced in herself and others a whole constellation of negative traits: jealousy, theft, dishonesty, lust, cowardice, brutality, infidelity, apathy, and rage. Above all, Mary Magdalen's selling of herself betrayed one of God's sweetest and most precious gifts—the gift of human sexuality that he entrusts to each one of us.

In the beautiful book *Covenant of Love*, Fathers Richard M. Hogan and John M. LeVoir point out that sexuality is a window to each person's very heart. When a married couple love each other in and through their sexual powers they become more and more what they truly are: images of God. Created in that image, we are only happy and at home with ourselves when we love as God loves; and Christ showed us at his crucifixion that his love is forever, it is fruitful, it is faithful, and it is a total self gift.

Even a woman unschooled in that truth senses it deep within herself. Mary Magdalen's pattern of counterfeit loves must have weighed on her heart like a stone. She was a great deal like ourselves in our own sins—torn, divided, restless, but caught in a web. The day she first heard Christ speaking about the kingdom of heaven, we imagine she must have come close to fainting with joy. No one anywhere, ever, had told her those things. Had a multitude of Biblical scholars scolded her, she never would have been moved to change. But the flesh and blood presence of Incarnate Love was like a blinding, beautiful light of hope.

Jesus melted Mary's heart because he invited her, and all of us, to embody the vision of his parables. When he told the crowds of Jerusalem about the Shepherd's loving search for the lost lamb, about the unfathomable value of the treasure in the field, and about the love showered on the prodigal son, he was speaking our language. He was reassuring all of us that he takes us as we are, where we are, no matter what we have done.

This is the kind of unconditional love that frees a sinner to change. Mary Magdalen could never have given up her livelihood unless she had something better to replace it with. Christ's faithful, forever, fruitful, and total self gift was her bridge back to happiness, beauty, truth, joy, and love. In asking her to give up all the prosperity her lifestyle had built, he was actually unlocking the door of a dungeon and setting her free.

Not all of us are wayward sexually or viewed as a public disgrace. But Mary Magdalen can still be, for every one of us, a personal touchstone of God's grace. He showed us through one woman's conversion that the power of his love is stronger and more powerful than the worst sins we have ever committed or ever will commit. His forgiveness is immediate and complete the moment we are sorry. And grace can do miracles in undoing the knots of sadness, loneliness, and negative traits we have caused by our sins.

If we ever question whether our sins are a barrier to intimacy with Christ, we can look to the fact that the day our Lord rose gloriously alive from the tomb the first person he sought was not Peter, the Rock of his Church, not John the beloved Apostle, not Mary his mother. The person he first approached and called by name was the once wild mistress of Magdala whose sins had been as scarlet. She who had followed him even to the foot of his Cross, who had wept at his death, and laid pungent spices in his burial cloths. She who had swung 180 degrees from sinner to saint.

Mary Magdalen's crucible of suffering became the most challenging after Jesus left this earth. The temptations arising from a scarred reputation, the misunderstanding of others, and turning her back daily on old ways could not have been easy. But believing Christ was invisibly but powerfully alive and close, Mary successfully handled her temptations in much the same way she did at the house of Simon. She took them straight to Jesus. She poured out her sorrows, needs, vulnerabilities, and love. And over and over again, he blessed her, forgave her, and filled her with grace on her way.

If Mary Magdalen, the misfit of Jerusalem, achieved glory in the kingdom of God, then we can too, by believing that our hope is not in ourselves, but in Jesus. Mary Magdalen could have fallen into a black hole of despair like Judas, but she chose to look not so much at her own weakness, but at Jesus' strength. She let him lift her up again. And God wanted the message of her life to reach all of us, because he said, "Wherever this Gospel shall be preached in the whole world, that also which she hast done shall be told for a memory of her" (Mt 26:13).

The Sorrowful Mysteries of the Rosary

1. *The Agony in the Garden:* The thought of our sins and his coming suffering causes the agonizing Savior to sweat blood (Lk 22:39–44).

2. *The Scourging:* Jesus is stripped and unmercifully scourged until his body is one mass of bloody wounds (Mt 27:26).

3. *The Crowning with Thorns:* Jesus' claim to kingship is ridiculed by putting a crown of thorns on his head and a reed in his hand (Mt 27:28–31).

4. *The Carrying of the Cross:* Jesus shoulders his own cross and carries it to the place of crucifixion while Mary follows him, sorrowing (Lk 23:26–32).

5. *The Crucifixion:* Jesus is nailed to the cross and dies after three hours of agony witnessed by his Mother (Mt 27:33–50).

Meditation on the Sorrowful Mysteries of the Rosary is recommended for Tuesdays and Fridays and for Sundays during Lent.

The

Glorious Mysteries

Of Being a Woman

Of the Church

On Being a Woman
of the Church

A convert from an atheistic though Jewish background, for me the basic realities of our Church have always seemed glorious.

Because I realize that some Catholics baptized as babies are more likely than I to take these mysteries for granted, a great deal of my apostolate has been in the area of teaching.

As we begin to ponder the glorious mysteries of being a woman of the Church, I would like to start with a prayer:

> God the Father, Creator of heaven and earth, God the Son, our Redeemer, God the Holy Spirit, our Sanctifier, Blessed Mary our Mother, and all the women saints, I pray that you may come to us now that we may exult in our vocation and destiny as women of the Church.

The Sacraments
of the Church

How beautiful are the sacraments of the Catholic Church. I think of them as inventions of Christ's love, ways that he found to come within us in a sensory manner, so that we would not feel abandoned when he left this earth. Just as a lover does not only give gifts of jewelry, flowers, or books, but especially wants to give his very self, so does Jesus, our eternal lover, want to give his very self to us by means of sacraments and prayer. I think of baptism as his first kiss; Communion as similar to the marital act of union; confirmation as his way of joining us to the Spirit of God in contrast to the worldly spirit which threatens to engulf us; confession as his way to assuage the wounds that come from our betrayal of him; holy orders as the chosen image of his sacrificial love for the Church; marriage as his way of supernaturalizing the bond of love; and anointing as the embrace a spouse would give his desperately ill companion to heal or strengthen her, as a last kiss before the journey to our eternal home.

The following are further insights, prayers, poems, and reflections on the wondrous mysteries which are the sacraments of the Church.

180

The Blessings of Baptism

1. An application of the merits of Christ.
2. A change into a new creature.
3. The remission of sins in general.
4. The remission of original sin and personal sin.
5. The remission of temporal punishment.
6. The conferring of grace.
7. Adoption into the sonship of God.
8. Regeneration.
9. The infusion of virtues.
10. Union with Christ, whose member the baptized person is made.
11. Liberation from the power of the devil.
12. The conferring of the gifts of the Holy Spirit (wisdom, understanding, knowledge, counsel, fortitude, piety, fear of the Lord, Is 11:2–3).
13. The beginning of spiritual life.
14. Reception into the Church.
15. The opening of heaven (for that soul).
16. The imprinting of a character, sign, seal.
17. The obligation of preserving the law of Christ.
18. The power to persevere in the law of Christ.
19. Becoming an heir to the kingdom of heaven.
20. The right to receive all the other sacraments.
21. The indwelling of the Blessed Trinity.
22. The espousal of the soul to Christ.
23. Wedded bliss.
24. The assigning of a personal guardian angel.
25. The soul becomes the temple of the Blessed Trinity.
26. Adoption as a child of Mary—protection of the Motherhood of Mary.
27. Illumination of the soul.
28. Movement toward the ecstasy of contemplative prayer.

29. A right to the prayers of Mary, the angels, and the saints.
30. Membership in the family of God.
31. Living membership in the Mystical Body of Christ.
32. The soul becomes a praise of glory.
33. The angels in heaven rejoice.
34. The angels in heaven adore the Blessed Trinity present in the soul.
35. A miracle of grace occurs.
36. The soul is divinized.
37. The soul is changed into Christ. "I live, now not I; but Christ liveth in me. . ." (Gal 2:20).
38. The soul's time yields to eternity.
39. The soul becomes a terrestrial paradise.
40. The eternal happiness of the soul begins.
41. A second creation of the soul takes place.
42. The soul dies with Christ and is resurrected with Christ.
43. The soul is elevated from the natural to the supernatural life.
44. The soul participates in the Divine Nature.
45. The soul enters into a communion of love with God.
46. All the actions of the soul have a value which is truly divine.
47. The soul is consecrated to live in the love of the Father, in the imitation of the Son, and in full communion with the Holy Spirit.
48. Sanctifying grace is imparted and remains in the soul and does not depart unless deliberately rejected by the soul through sin of a mortal nature.
49. The soul participates in the Divine Essence.
50. A real "death and resurrection" occurs in the soul; death to the old Adam (original sin), death with

Christ on the Cross, and resurrection with Christ into the New Adam.

51. We are made priests and victims with Christ Jesus.

Phyllis Schabow

> Ample hemmed
> baptismal gown
> Mother Church
> will slowly let it
> down.
> In heaven
> it will be a perfect fit.

Ronda Chervin

My Prayer for a Priest
Especially at Christmas

May your consecration never be cold!
May you wonder with the Virgin
  as the Holy Spirit overshadows you,
May you see Jesus born in your hands
  as truly as he was born in the stable.
May the hosts of angels
  who sang his welcome then,
  assist you in welcoming him now—and
May you see the faithful as the shepherds,
  the special guests—invited by
  God himself—to witness this wonder.
May the warm life of the precious Blood
  burn your hands—and your heart—
  as you touch the chalice
May your consecration never be cold!

Alice M. Sava

Prayer for Priests

O Jesus, Eternal High Priest, keep thy priests within the
shelter of thy Sacred Heart, where none may touch
them.

Keep unstained their anointed hands, which daily touch
thy Sacred Body.

Keep unsullied their lips, daily purpled with thy Precious
Blood.

Keep pure and unworldly their hearts, sealed with the
sacred character of the priesthood.

Let thy holy love surround them from the world's con-
tagion.

Bless their labors with abundant fruit, and may the souls
to whom they minister be their joy and consolation
here on earth and their everlasting crown hereafter in
heaven. Amen.

Linda Helminiak

The Mass brings the sad world to immediacy and enables
me to be compassionate just by loving thoughts. Better
than space travel.

Fr. John Winson, Australia

When I approached to receive Communion and recalled
that extraordinary majesty I had seen (in a vision) and
considered that it was present in the Blessed Sacrament
(the Lord often desires that I behold it in the host), my hair
stood on end; the whole experience seemed to annihilate
me. O my Lord! If you did not hide your grandeur, who
would approach so often a union of something so dirty
and miserable with such great majesty! May the angels
and all creatures praise you, for you so measure things in
accordance with our weakness that when we rejoice in
your sovereign favors your great power does not so
frighten us that, as weak and wretched people, we would
not dare to enjoy them.

Teresa of Avila

I wish that every Catholic who can possibly do so would attend daily Mass. It is such a blessing, such a way to be centered in his Heart.

It is motherly of Christ to want to come right into us as our food in the Eucharist. Like a mother he feels frustrated when a guest refuses his food. During the hearings on the Concerns of Women for the Bishops' Pastoral on that subject, the Eucharist came up again and again as what was most important for Catholics in being part of the Church.

As our Holy Father, Pope John Paul II, writes so exquisitely in his encyclical *Redemptor Hominis*:

> In this sacrament . . . he entrusts himself to us with limitless trust, as if not taking into consideration our human weakness, our unworthiness, the force of habit, routine, or even the possibility of insult. Every member of the Church . . . must be vigilant in seeing that this sacrament of love should be the center of the life of the people of God—(so that) Christ should be given back "love for love" and truly become the life of our souls.

Mary Collette Anderson describes her move to Idaho in this inspiring way:

> We are moving to Twin Falls, Idaho, right into Mormon country. How I panicked at first. But now I see that maybe I am meant to do our Lady's work there. What has strengthened me is the parish there, Saint Edwards . . . the parents have reopened the school after a five year death. This tiny parish has twenty-four hour adoration —I saw it with my own eyes. It has been exposed there and never unguarded for the last four years. The Prisoner is out. Graces pour down on this place. I could feel it

when I visited. I was fully prepared to hate the place as I am one of nine of an Irish Catholic entrenched Denver family. We are going to farm, simply live our lives and give the children a deep love for our Blessed Lord in the Eucharist. . . .

Perhaps some readers are being called to initiate Perpetual Adoration in their own parishes.

A General Communion

I saw the throng, so deeply separate,
    Fed at one only board—
The devout people, moved, intent, elate,
    And the devoted Lord.

O struck apart! not side from human side,
    But soul from human soul,
As each asunder absorbed the multiplied,
    The ever unparted, whole.

I saw this people as a field of flowers,
    Each grown at such a price
The sum of unimaginable powers
    Did no more than suffice.

A thousand single central daisies they,
    A thousand of the one;
For each, the entire monopoly of day;
    For each, the whole of the devoted sun.

Alice Meynell

Mary Divulet, a Marian Woman, mentions the practice of Saint Louis Marie de Montfort in his wonderful book *True Devotion* (a book much loved by the Holy Father) of receiving Jesus in union with Mary in the Eucharist:

After Holy Communion, inwardly recollected and holding your eyes shut, you will introduce Jesus into the heart of Mary. You will give him to his Mother, who will receive him honorably, will adore him profoundly, will love him perfectly, will embrace him closely, and will render to him, in spirit and in truth, many homages which are unknown to us in our thick darkness.

And here is such an incisive passage about the sacrament of confession by Pascal:

The Catholic religion does not bind us to confess our sins indiscriminately to everybody; it allows them to remain hidden from all other men save one, to whom she bids us reveal the innermost recesses of our heart and to show ourselves as we are. There is only this one man in the world whom she orders us to undeceive, and she binds him to an inviolable secrecy, which makes this knowledge to him as if it were not. Can we imagine anything more charitable and pleasant? And yet the corruption of man is such that he finds even this law harsh; and it is one of the main reasons which has caused a great part of Europe to rebel against the Church.

How unjust and unreasonable is the heart of man, which feels it disagreeable to be obliged to do in regard to one man what in some measure it were right to do to all men! For is it right that we should deceive men? . . .

It is this false delicacy which makes those who are under the necessity of reproving others choose so many windings and middle courses to avoid offence. They must lessen our faults, appear to excuse them, intersperse praises and evidence of love and esteem. Despite all this, the medicine does not cease to be bitter to self-love. It takes a little as it can, always with disgust, and often with a secret spite against those who administer it.

. . . and a very feminine reflection by Alice M. Sava:

Today I mended an alb for Jesus. It's hem was soiled and torn from following him as he healed the maimed, gave sight to the blind, opened the ears of the deaf, gave love to the unloved and unloving.

My soul, too, is soiled and torn—from running away from him, from maiming self and others, from blinding self and others, from shutting the ears of self and others, from hiding Love from the unloved and unloving.

As my love for him mended this alb so that his priest may wear it to continue his Mass—I prayed that his love for me would mend my soul so that I may wear it to make my life a Mass.

The Prayer of the Church

I have written quite a few books on prayer. It is one of my favorite subjects. As a convert from an atheistic background, what a fantastic moment it was for me to realize that I could converse with God!

There are so many ways to pray—asking God for what we need in vocal prayer, giving him thanks, praise for his glory, contrition prayer, the rosary, meditating on the Bible, deep wordless contemplative prayer of quiet, the Jesus prayer repeating his name over and over again, singing hymns, sacred dancing, writing to God, and listening to his words in our hearts.

In this brief introduction to prayer I am going to highlight only two types of prayer: meditating on Scripture and charismatic prayer, for these may be the ones least familiar to some readers. I will also include a description of how to pray the rosary (for some find these simple instructions hard to come by), and some other Marian prayers.

Meditating on Scripture

For meditating on Scripture, here is a beautifully written description by Marian Woman Dana Black:

SPEAK LORD,
YOUR SERVANT IS LISTENING

A few years ago, a close friend shared with me the frustration and confusion she experienced in her conversion to the Catholic Faith. Her desire for God soared into the heavens, but her understanding of how to proceed remained anchored to earth. At every turn, she found herself thwarted with disordered opinions and discrepancies in teachings. Mountains upon mountains of books, periodicals, and tapes were available as learning tools. As the materials became more and more accessible, her bewilderment groaned within her. A soul wounded by a desire for God was ensnared by pages of opinions, methods, and insights. All she wanted was God. She turned to me for help, but I, too, was uncertain which of the many paths in the maze was the right one. . . . Suddenly we realized the perfect source for guidance in the spiritual life is the Bible.

What we stumbled upon has been very much a part of Church teaching for years. Saint Thérèse of Lisieux relied on Saint John of the Cross, *The Imitation of Christ*, and the Gospels for her spiritual direction. Both Saint John of the Cross and Thomas à Kempis were radically dependent upon Sacred Scripture in their writings which illuminated the way through this world to union with God. . . .

Saint Jerome wrote, "Ignorance of Scripture is ignorance of Christ." Saint Jerome believed that we have to know the word of God in order to live it.

The practice of prayerful reading, reflection, and assimilation of Sacred Scripture is called *Lectio Divina*. After Jesus' Ascension and the hearing of the word through the Apostles, the early Christians *listened to God revealing himself*: a reading from the Old Testament, a reading from the Apostles and a Gospel reading . . . as a natural prelude to the prayerful encounter with God in the Eucharist. His Spirit in the word prepares our hearts to be supernaturally open to the grace of the Blessed Sacrament. . . . As the prophets were for the Jews of the Old Testament, and the Apostles were for early Christians—the lectors today are for us.

Scriptures contain more than a thousand pages of in-depth, highly concentrated, heavily symbolized, historically rooted yet timeless, supernatural words, telling us about God and simultaneously being God's call to us. As we contemplate, we find ourselves faced with the numinous relational mystery of Christ and Scripture. . . .

Once a Catholic Bible has been selected, one must determine which course of perusal to take. Scripture can be encountered liturgically, in a thematic manner, from the viewpoint of a particular book or of a collected group of writings. We can make the liturgical readings the object of our prayer. This route is directed by the gentle and loving touch of Divine Wisdom, as he speaks to us through the Church. We are spared the mental clutter of being overloaded with excessive and unrelated biblical insights.

Before retiring for the evening, calmly scan the readings for the following day, renewing freshly the gospel truth. After prayerful consideration and reflection, you will find that some portion of the word usually speaks to you personally in your life as you find it today. Inner contemplation then often expresses the conformity of our lives to the gospel call, and we are uplifted in a cloud of placid gratitude. On other days, we discern a growth message, when our egocentric desires are out of harmony with God's will and God's word. Daily readings will speak to us of his will. We listen and pray that our mentality and our lives may be brought into accord with the scriptural way. . . .

Another way is to follow themes with the assistance of a concordance collecting readings on peace, love, joy, patience, gratitude, humility, mercy, gentleness, holiness, or prayer. We could also gather readings on wisdom, women, or specific individuals. Or you may select a specific book.

Scripture is a supernatural food which nourishes the soul. We are weak, blind, and often dumb creatures when it comes to spiritual vision. We need not only sacramental, but also scriptural sustenance. . . .

Charismatic Prayer

In the course of giving workshops and lectures in parishes throughout the world, I have found that many Catholics who did not become acquainted with the charismatic gifts of the Holy Spirit in the sixties and seventies have become interested at this time. I would like to say just a bit about how these gifts were offered to me, for it is certainly the case that God has chosen this way to increase the fervor of the prayer life and communal love of many in a manner they have not found elsewhere.

It was the summer of 1969. I was living in San Juan Capistrano, a small mission town in California. Hoping that the temperate climate might improve my husband's worsening asthma condition, our family had moved there from New York City.

For me, it was a time of crisis. My husband's health had deteriorated so badly that he could no longer carry on his work as president of a world-wide book distribution company. Our five-year-old twin daughters were about to start kindergarten. I had planned not to work full time until my children were teenagers, but under the circumstances I was very glad that my husband insisted I finish my doctorate in philosophy and take up a regular teaching job.

In September I was to begin commuting to Los Angeles, sixty-seven miles away, to take up the position of assistant professor of philosophy at Loyola University. My husband was to spend six months at the National Jewish Hospital in Denver, Colorado—a last-ditch attempt at a cure.

Before my husband's trip to Denver and my own first full-time teaching job, my twin sister, Carla De Sola, came to visit us during the summer. Carla was bubbling over with the strange news that she had received the gift of tongues!

You can understand why I so easily dismissed her experience when I explained that I was and still am what might be called a very conservative Catholic. A convert to the Catholic Faith from a Jewish though atheistic background, I cling with tremendous fervor to the Church which is to me a light shining in the darkness.

At that time I particularly loved my daily Latin Mass. Each day I prayed the rosary for the conversion of my husband, practiced special devotions to the saints, and used all the intellectual power at my command to defend the doctrines of Catholicism against all doubters within and without the Church. I had an excellent spiritual guide to whom I submitted theological problems which arose, and I was totally averse to anything innovative unless it had been approved officially by Rome. With this in mind, you can imagine with what enthusiasm I greeted the announcement of my convert-sister that she was involved in a crazy new movement in the Church which claimed the gift of glossolalia (speaking in tongues)!

My sister's visit was to last most of the summer, spanning her teaching assignment at Saint Joseph's College of Orange. So I decided not to pounce on her immediately with refutations of the gift of tongues. I decided to read up on the subject and marshal the best possible arguments. But materials about the movement were almost nonexistent, and my sister, a very peaceful and charming person, did not argue with me or try to push her new spirituality on me. So I tried to push the subject into the back of my mind. I love my sister dearly and I was eager to avoid an open confrontation.

However, very gently Carla would ask me one question which became a real annoyance: "Ronda, how do you express your closeness to the Holy Spirit?"

In spite of glaring faults, I regarded myself as an exemplary Catholic. But I had to confess that, to me, the Holy Spirit was more of a concept than a living Person. I also had difficulty believing that praying in tongues could go on in our times. I was of the opinion that the gift of tongues, a gift once given to the Apostles for conveying the gospel to people from many countries, was now defunct.

This background will help to explain why I could never regard the experience which was soon to follow as a natural result of my sister's influence or of mass psychology.

One evening after the children were in bed, and my husband had left for the clinic in Denver, I was alone with my sister. We were listening to a favorite piece of music on my husband's superb stereo equipment. The piece was the Bach B Minor Mass with its sublime crescendo of brass instruments proclaiming the "cum Sancto Spiritu" of the Gloria. I had always delighted in this particular movement. But I had never fully understood why a composer would select the coming of the Holy Spirit, to me a mere concept, for such ecstatic treatment.

At the peak of the victorious trumpet blasts when the singers intoned "cum Sancto Spiritu", I looked at my sister. To my amazement, her face had become transformed, as it were, into the face of Jesus! Unknown to herself it seemed as if the humble, merciful, loving countenance of Christ, as depicted by such artists as Rembrandt and El Greco, shone through her normal features. Drawn into the aura of this totally unexpected vision I said without any forethought: "Whatever you want to do to me about the Holy Spirit, go ahead!"

Surprised and somewhat dismayed—for she had little experience of the laying on of hands—Carla did place her hands on my head and prayed very, very softly. A tremendous flood of love and strength and happiness enveloped me and then some syllables in a strange language started coming into my mind. By then, it was rather late and I went to bed in a sort of daze.

When I awoke, I practically leaped out of bed for joy and all day long I felt on fire with love of God. The fire of the Spirit filled me with a soft, subtle, abiding sense of the dove-like presence of God within me. This quiet indwelling of the Spirit was something I had known before, but only as a fleeting grace. The great truths of the Faith which I had always believed now seemed illumined and blazing with power. I could hardly wait to proclaim them afresh—not as intellectual doctrines, but as burning realities.

Ever since my sister prayed over me that night for the release of the Spirit, the quiet sense of God's loving presence has been with me.

I also received many gifts for ministry as a teacher and in prayer groups and came to love the warm open atmosphere of prayerful caring I found in other charismatics.

Praying the Rosary

My favorite kind of prayer at this time of my life is quiet prayer of simplicity, opening my heart to receive the love of Christ and to listen to his words within. And yet the rosary is seldom away from my hand when I am at prayer. I find it the best preparation for contemplative prayer.

I came to love the rosary in a strange manner. A friend of mine was boasting about how her husband was converted after she made a vow to pray the rosary every day for the rest of her life. Since my husband was still an unbeliever I hastily made the same vow!

At first it was a strain to say it, but after awhile, instead of finding it boring, I began to experience deep comfort. Later on, I wrote a book with Sister Mary Neill called *Bringing the Mother with You: Healing Meditations on the Mysteries of Mary*. I learned how to meditate on the themes of each mystery and weave into them my own life story of joys, sorrows, and glories. Much given to melancholy brooding or roller-coaster elation, it is very calming for me to realize that the rhythm of delight and sadness is part of our life in Christ. Mary teaches me how to ponder the joy to deepen it and how to identify my sufferings with those of Christ. The glorious mysteries are marvelous glimpses to me of the future which awaits me. To think that one day I, too, will have a perfect, grace-filled body in heaven and will be crowned with God's rewards for fighting the good fight through thick and thin, mostly thick!

Cardinal Ratzinger writes that "if the rosary is prayed as tradition envisages it draws us into a rhythm of calm which makes us flexible and well-balanced, giving a name to this peace: Jesus, the blessed fruit of Mary."

The basic way of praying the rosary given here is not the only way. Variations go from simply letting the beads slide through one's fingers while saying Hail Marys and Our Fathers, to the scriptural meditations that can be related to each mystery in a small book called the *Scriptural Rosary*.

HOW TO SAY THE ROSARY

Start with the *Sign of the Cross* and the *Apostles' Creed*, then the *Our Father* on the large bead, the *Hail Mary* on each of the three small beads, and add the *Glory Be*.

Choose a set of Mysteries to meditate on. Think about the first Mystery while you pray the *Our Father* on the large bead, the *Hail Mary* on each of the following ten small beads, and then add the *Glory Be*. This is called a decade of the rosary. Think about the second Mystery while you pray the next decade: *Our Father*, *Hail Mary* ten times, and *Glory Be*.

You can stop after any decade and pick it up later at the next decade. Your rosary has five decades, and the Mysteries come in groups of five. That's the usual amount for a day. But you can use all fifteen Mysteries and go around the rosary three times, if you wish.

PRAYERS OF THE ROSARY

In the name of the Father, and of the Son, and of the Holy Spirit, Amen.

The Apostles' Creed

I believe in God, the Father Almighty, Creator of heaven and earth; and in Jesus Christ, his only Son, our Lord; who was conceived by the Holy Spirit, born of the Virgin Mary, suffered under Pontius Pilate, was crucified, died and was buried. He descended into hell; the third day he rose again from the dead; he ascended into heaven, is seated at the right hand of God, the Father Almighty; from thence he shall come to judge the living and the dead. I believe in the Holy Spirit, the holy Catholic Church, the communion of saints, the forgiveness of sins, the resurrection of the body, and life everlasting. Amen.

The Our Father

Our Father, who art in heaven, hallowed be thy name, thy kingdom come; thy will be done on earth as it is in heaven. Give us this day our daily bread; and forgive us our trespasses, as we forgive those who trespass against us. And lead us not into temptation; but deliver us from evil. Amen.

The Hail Mary

Hail, Mary, full of grace; the Lord is with thee; blessed art thou among women, and blessed is the fruit of thy womb, Jesus. Holy Mary, Mother of God, pray for us sinners, now and at the hour of our death. Amen.

The Glory Be to the Father

Glory be to the Father, and to the Son, and to the Holy Spirit. As it was in the beginning, is now, and ever shall be, world without end. Amen.

For the meditations on the Joyful Mysteries of the Rosary, see p. 98; for the Sorrowful Mysteries, see p. 175; and for the Glorious Mysteries, see p. 255 of this book.

Other Marian Prayers

The Magnificat

My soul proclaims the greatness of the Lord,
my spirit rejoices in God my Savior
for he has looked with favor on his lowly servant.

From this day all generations will call me blessed:
the Almighty has done great things for me,
and holy is his Name.

He has mercy on those who fear him
in every generation.

He has shown the strength of his arm,
he has scattered the proud in their conceit.

He has cast down the mighty from their thrones,
and has lifted up the lowly.

He has filled the hungry with good things,
and the rich he has sent away empty.

He has come to the help of his servant Israel
for he has remembered his promise of mercy,
the promise he made to our fathers,
to Abraham and his children forever.

An Our Mother Prayer
for the Assumption

Our Mother who has been raised into heaven, blessed be
your name. Your reign extend on earth as it does in
heaven. This day as you fed him the food of your body,
feed us the food of his Body. Pray for forgiveness for us
and for our forgiving of others, as you heard him do from

the cross. Lead us along his way by helping us to remember your last words "do what he tells you". And, please do not forget your children, O Maria.

George Wunderlick

Litany of the Blessed Virgin

Lord, have mercy on us.
Christ, have mercy on us.
Lord, have mercy on us.
Christ, hear us.
Christ, graciously hear us.
God the Father of heaven, *have mercy on us.*
God the Son, Redeemer of the world, *have mercy on us.*
God the Holy Spirit, *have mercy on us.*
Holy Trinity, one God, *have mercy on us.*
Holy Mary, *pray for us.*
Holy Mother of God, . . .
Holy Virgin of virgins, . . .
Mother of Christ, . . .
Mother of divine grace, . . .
Mother most pure, . . .
Mother most chaste, . . .
Mother inviolate, . . .
Mother undefiled, . . .
Mother most amiable, . . .
Mother most admirable, . . .
Mother of good counsel, . . .
Mother of our Creator, . . .
Mother of our Savior, . . .
Virgin most prudent, . . .
Virgin most venerable, . . .
Virgin most renowned, . . .
Virgin most powerful, . . .
Virgin most merciful, . . .

Virgin most faithful, . . .
Mirror of justice, . . .
Seat of wisdom, . . .
Cause of our joy, . . .
Spiritual vessel, . . .
Vessel of honor, . . .
Singular vessel of devotion, . . .
Mystical rose, . . .
Tower of David, . . .
Tower of ivory, . . .
House of gold, . . .
Ark of the covenant, . . .
Gate of heaven, . . .
Morning star, . . .
Health of the sick, . . .
Refuge of sinners, . . .
Comforter of the afflicted, . . .
Help of Christians, . . .
Queen of angels, . . .
Queen of confessors, . . .
Queen of virgins, . . .
Queen of all saints, . . .
Queen conceived without original sin, . . .
Queen of the most holy rosary, . . .
Queen assumed into heaven, . . .
Queen of peace, . . .

Lamb of God, who takest away the sins of the world,
spare us, O Lord.
Lamb of God, who takest away the sins of the world,
graciously hear us, O Lord.
Lamb of God, who takes away the sins of the world,
have mercy on us.
Christ hear us,
Christ graciously hear us.

V. Pray for us, O holy Mother of God.

R. That we may be made worthy of the promises of Christ.

Let us pray. Grant unto us, thy servants, we beseech thee, O Lord God, at all times to enjoy health of soul and body; and by the glorious intercession of Blessed Mary, ever virgin, when freed from the sorrows of this present life, to enter into that joy which hath no end. Through Christ our Lord. *R. Amen.*

Women in Ministry

Sometimes I think that if I am not womanly in all possible ways, I am a failure. It has helped me very much to study types of femininity in order to realize that I am very strong as a woman in some ways, but weaker in others. I see that God has graced me in some ways, but there are other paths I have hardly explored.

Here is a description of some womanly paths. I have described them as ministries. That is a just a different way of talking about the old corporal and spiritual works of mercy, as a friend of mine remarked.

As you read this, and other writings in *Woman to Woman*, you might want to keep a journal in the margin or in a notebook. If you have a friend or a group reading this book together, you could share your experiences in each section and then pray about ways you want to grow.

The Motherly Ministry

Women of the motherly type, whether we are biologically mothers or not, besides being good at raising children, are usually good at mothering anyone in need because of our great empathy.

Most women receptionists at the rectory are motherly

in nature, and so are counselors, teachers of small children, nurses, and many women in other professions.

How do you react to the needs of those around you? If you want to flee, then you are probably not the motherly type. If you rush forward, then you are. Famous women with a motherly ministry include Saint Ann, Saint Elizabeth of Hungary, Saint Margaret of Castello, Saint Elizabeth Seton, Mother Teresa of Calcutta, and many others.

Mary, as Mother of God and Mother of the Church is also, of course, a motherly minister. Beautiful nativity paintings present us with Mary as an archetype of the nobility of motherhood. The image of Mary, cloak extended, sheltering legions of weak sinners, is also a moving invitation to come to her maternal arms.

The Prophetic Ministry

Women who love to challenge complacency and mediocrity as well as sinful patterns in society, have a prophetic ministry.

Does the sight of evil make you want to retreat or to fight? If it makes you want to do anything possible to remedy the situation, then you probably have a gift for prophetic ministry. It is in this category that we find the women prophetesses of the Old Testament, the women doctors of the Church, Teresa of Avila and Catherine of Siena, Joan of Arc, many foundresses and modern leaders such as those working for pro-life causes, and many others.

Mary of the apparitions is often revealed as a truly prophetic woman in her denunciation of sin and calling forth of penance.

The Creative Ministry

Creative women of the Church tend to be motivated by the lack of beauty they find in the areas of music, art, dance, and also human interaction. They want to improve these situations by adding the beauty that will overcome drabness. Gifted with spontaneity, such women are better at doing a particular work for the Church rather than handling details as an administrator would do. Creative free-spirited women make wonderful hostesses and greeters, for they are not worried about scheduling in such a way as to put time above human contact.

One of my most vivid images of a creative woman in ministry is Maria as portrayed in *Sound of Music*. I think of Mother Angelica as having a creative type of womanly ministry. I also imagine Saint Clare and Julian of Norwich as having such gifts. Catholic women writers such as Alice Meynell, Sigrid Undset, Caryll Houselander, and Flannery O'Connor can be described as women in the creative ministry.

A liturgy for the Blessed Virgin has her fulfilling the prophecy of one who would play before God. Some scholars suggest that many of the delightful images and parables of Jesus were given to him in his early years by his mother.

The Interior Ministry

Sometimes so much emphasis is placed on motherly ministries concerning corporal works of mercy, or on the publicity that prophetic women get, we can lose sight of the tremendous ministry in our Church that comes from women of prayer. The interior woman tries first to find a path into her own soul, to the place of peace where our Eucharistic Lord is to be found waiting for us to meet him. The joy of her discovery leads her to want to minister to others in prayer, especially to those who have not found a way to peace.

Some holy women of deep interiority are Saint Gertrude, Saint Thérèse of Lisieux, Saint Jane de Chantal, Saint Bernadette. Our Lady of Solitude, and all the titles of Mary showing her to be the mother of intercession and contemplation, make her our primary model of the woman who ponders the graces of the Holy Spirit in her heart.

Spiritual Motherhood

I carry you under my heart,
a soft heavy presence
slowing my steps.
I smile mysteriously
like a woman with child—
only other God-bearers understand.

Ronda Chervin

I Would Like to Imitate

Her simplicity
   and shun all affectations and pretense
Her humility
   and erase all pride I use in my defense
Her charity
   and give love in abundance and in excess
Her serenity
   and be calm amidst chaos and distress
Her understanding
   and listen with kind heart to those who complain
Her kindness
   and offer comfort to those in pain
Her patience
   and endure all that is ill
Her obedience
   and bow my head to God's all-holy will.

I would like to imitate her every day. Please God make me more and more like your blessed Mother Mary, I pray.

Dolores Valladares

Prayer for
Marian Women in Ministry

Our Lady, Queen of Apostles, show us, your daughters, how to become the handmaids of the Lord in his Church. May we exult in our Savior, that his love may flow in us and through us to those in need of our ministry.

Catholic Faith, Hope, and Love

Faith

Many Catholic women I meet are troubled by the diversity of opinions current in our times about matters of faith. On the one hand they meet unbelievers and confused Christians who think that all that matters is to "lead a good life" and no longer think that specific Catholic doctrines are that important. On the other hand, they meet fundamentalists who question anything that does not have a crystal clear reference in the Bible—their version of the Bible.

In view of this situation, instead of giving beautiful quotations about faith, I thought it would be more profitable to include in this chapter short answers to questions commonly asked about Catholic teachings, written by Terri Vorndran Nichols:

QUICK ANSWERS TO QUESTIONS ABOUT THE CATHOLIC FAITH

Sunday Mass, frequent reception of the sacraments:

What is the necessity of attending Sunday Mass, when I can be close to God in the silence of my heart, *wherever* I go?

Truly, we are temples of the Holy Spirit and God is with us always. But something happens at every Mass that brings God's presence even closer.

The Mass is not a church service which Catholics attend and watch. The Mass is an action, something Catholics *do* together. At every Mass Catholics join to re-enact what Jesus himself did, and what he asked us to do, on the night before he died. There, in the company of his disciples at the Last Supper he took the bread, blessed it, broke it, gave it to them and said: "Take this, all of you, and eat it: this is my body which will be given up for you." When supper was ended, he took the cup, gave it to his disciples, and said: "Take this, all of you, and drink from it: this is the cup of my blood, the blood of the new and everlasting covenant . . . *do this in memory of me.*"

His request that Passover night has been obeyed without interruption for nearly 2,000 years.

So what does the Mass have to offer that a rich spiritual conversation with friends or a good meditative walk in the woods doesn't?

The Mass alone gives us the Eucharist, the bread of life of which Jesus promised, "He who eats this bread shall never die." Every time we receive the Eucharist at Mass, Christ comes inside our hearts—not in a figurative or symbolic way—but really and truly, fully alive. We are taking Christ at his word when we believe and embrace this mystery.

During that heart to heart time with Christ after receiving Holy Communion, a lot of incalculably wonderful things happen. He floods our souls with grace. He helps us to overcome faults and difficulties. He forgives and washes away our sins. He unites us with one another and helps us to love as he loves. In short, he actually makes us one with himself. This is as close as we will ever get to him on this earth. It is a foretaste of heaven. Even the angels themselves cannot receive this privilege. The Eucharist is a gift of God's special bond with mankind. Who wants to forfeit a treasure like that!

When people say they "don't get anything out of Mass",

they are missing the point. We do not go to Mass just to "get" something; we go to give something back. It takes faith and love to attend Mass. Sometimes it takes time that is very precious—say, if we are studying or traveling or just need extra sleep. But the mystery and beauty of Mass is that we always end up gaining much more than we give: grace, peace of heart, the family support of a Catholic community.

Confession, sacramental value:

Why do I have to tell my sins to someone else when my sins are between me and God?

On Easter night when Jesus appeared to the apostles he said to them: "Peace be with you. As the Father has sent me, so I send you." Then he breathed on them and said, "Receive the Holy Spirit. If you forgive men's sins they are forgiven them; if you hold them bound, they are held bound" (Jn 20:21–23). With these and other words, Jesus gave his promise that he would forgive our sins through his priestly representative on earth. When the priest absolves our sins, it is Christ who is really forgiving us through him. Yes, our sins *are* between us and God, but God gave us the sacrament of penance, or reconciliation, for several wise reasons.

First, he has perfect understanding of the needs of the human heart. He knows that when we carry around a sorrow or sense of shame, it helps us to confide it to another person. Once the priest hears our problems and worries, he is in a good position to counsel us. Moreover, confession gives us a concrete reassurance that God has actually forgiven us. There is a tangible peace that comes over us when we have unloaded our conscience and received the blessing and Sign of the Cross in absolution.

Confession also is valuable because, in telling another person our faults and sins, we must face them ourselves. We do not bury them, but bring them to light and free ourselves.

Remember the prodigal son. He felt sorry in his heart. But he could not rest until he went before his father and asked aloud for pardon. The father blessed the repentant son for doing so, and gave him a fresh start.

Ordination to the priesthood:

Why is the priesthood the province of men when women are equally valuable in the sight of God?

The Church clearly proclaims the equal dignity of women and men, and invites both to serve the people of God.

The enduring tradition of a male *priesthood*, however, traces back to the birth of the Church when Jesus called the first Twelve, all men, to carry out his priestly mission. Among the many holy women that accompanied the itinerant Jesus, not one was called to this early priesthood.

Many argue that this exclusivity was due to the social circumstances of ancient Jerusalem; 2,000 years ago women were patently barred from roles of leadership—an archaic notion today.

A close look at the Gospels, however, will remind us that Jesus continually broke with the prejudices of his time, blatantly counteracting the discriminations practiced against women. By pardoning the woman taken in adultery (Jn 8:11), for example, Jesus held up a mirror to the faces of the Pharisees, teaching that one must not be more severe toward the sin of a woman than toward that of a man—that double standards are unjust.

Again, in the Gospels of Mark (10:2–11) and Matthew (19:3–9), Jesus challenges Mosaic Law in affirming the equality of rights and duties of women and men in the bond of marriage. Elsewhere in the Gospel (Jn 4:27) he shocked his own followers by sitting and conversing publicly with the Samaritan woman. Similarly (Lk 7:37) he scandalized the Pharisees at the house of Simon by accepting and blessing the uninvited presence of a very public prostitute.

No, Jesus was not prejudiced against women.

Sacramental ordination is extended to men and not to women, *not* because women are second-class citizens in the

Church, but because the Lord of the Church called men to that role. Christianity has always held that neither sex is better than the other, just different—and with the differences come special powers. Only women, for example, can bear new life.

When God chose to reveal himself, he did so by the taking on of human flesh by the Second Person of the Blessed Trinity as God's *son*. The symbolic value of the priest's maleness is an image of Christ, who in turn is an image of the Father. We have to remember that the Eucharistic liturgy is a special cultic act in which the material signs must resemble closely what is signified; bread and wine, for example, cannot be substituted with crackers and grape juice. It is for the male priest to image Christ the Bridegroom in the action of the Mass.

Mary, the mother of God, who surpassed all the apostles in excellence and dignity, is a luminous model of feminine leadership for women in the Church today.

> She lives her womanhood as virgin, as mother, as bride, and as spouse. If she is recognized as the prototype of woman, then it becomes most evident how utterly absurd it would be to imagine Mary acting as a priest, perhaps preaching or even uttering the words of consecration. "Women, by looking to Mary, find in her the secret of living their femininity with dignity, and of achieving their own true advancement. In the light of Mary, the Church sees in the face of women the reflection of a beauty that mirrors the loftiest sentiments of which the human heart is capable: the self-offering totality of love; the strength that is capable of bearing the greatest sorrows; limitless fidelity and tireless devotion to work; the ability to combine penetrating intuition with words of comfort and encouragement" (*RM*, no. 46).[1]

---

[1] Hans Urs von Balthasar and John Paul II in *Mary, God's Yes to Man*: Pope John Paul II's encyclical *Redemptoris Mater* with an introduction by Cardinal Joseph Ratzinger and commentary by von Balthasar (Ignatius Press, 1988), p. 178.

Chastity before marriage:

> Why does the Church frown on the loving consummation
> of love outside of marriage—even when two people know
> they *will* be sharing their lives together?

C. S. Lewis once wrote that chastity has always been the most
unpopular of the Christian virtues. Indeed, for many, chastity
before marriage seems to have gone the way of the hand-
cranked Victrola or the Model T Ford.

An unmarried couple in love may reason that sexual fulfillment is a very compelling pleasure, that it brings them
closer, and that it has a natural and vital place in their budding
relationship.

They would be only half-right. Human sexuality, of course,
is good and beautiful and intended for pleasure; God invented
it to be that way. The physical attraction we feel toward the
opposite sex, our desires for sexual union, the pleasure received in intercourse—all this is part of our sexual nature as
God created it. "Therefore shall a man leave his father and
mother, and shall cleave unto his wife; and they shall be *one
flesh*" (Gen 2:17). Numerous passages in Scripture's Song of
Songs speak joyously of the ecstatic delight God intends for a
loving husband and wife.

So how can something so intrinsically good and noble after
marriage be wrong before marriage?

We must understand that intercourse is more than a physical
act between two bodies. The body, as God made it, is the
expression of the person. The act of lovemaking, then, is a
vivid physical expression of the total union between two
persons, body and soul. It is the husband's sign language to his
wife, and a wife's to her husband, that nothing is held back. In
other words, it is a tangible sign or seal of the self-surrender,
profound intimacy, and total union that are the very core of a
marriage covenant. Only in marriage do a man and a woman

pledge all of themselves to each other. Lovemaking is the sign of this total self-gift.

Sex is also ordered to the procreation of new human life. The concept of Catholic marriage includes this purpose as an integral part of the affection and lovemaking of a husband and wife. God made this sexual experience sacred, which is why indulgence outside of marriage profanes a sacred thing. Engaged Catholic couples who yearn to consummate their love before marriage can actually show a deeper, truer love and loyalty for each other by helping each other to stay chaste. Chastity keeps the more crucial premarital exploration of ideas, beliefs, values, dreams, and life goals from getting clouded. It is also the best preparation for fidelity in married life.

Celibacy and virginity in consecrated souls:

> How does this abstinence from a natural, God-given gift serve anyone or anything?

In the case of priests and religious, sacrificing the powers of sexuality is not to be seen as a denial of rights or a negative element. Rather it is the opposite—a positive and fruitful gift back to God. This is a mystery until we realize the inherent value of a consecrated life.

The priest, for example, is consecrated and empowered to be another Christ for the people of God. Jesus works through him to forgive sinners, to teach and preach, to give the divine life through the sacraments, to renew his sacrifice on the cross, and to be a special servant to the pilgrim Church. Because the priest devotes himself to the spiritual needs of many, he needs to be essentially free. In the words of one devout Jesuit, "A good priest is one who could pack his bags within fifteen minutes if called to the other side of the world." Sexuality, and the naturally associated wife and children that a priest might have, would be shortchanged as the priest was "on call" every day to preach, baptize, bless the sick, counsel other families, hear confessions, say the Mass, and many other acts of love 'round the calendar. The sacrifice of celibacy, on the other hand, becomes a positive bond between the priest, Christ, and his people. It enables a priest to be true to his commitment, by allowing him freer and broader expression of his priestly love.

In the case of religious, virginity is a positive choice of chastity and a sign of love and commitment to Christ. It makes the statement that one is giving oneself totally, relinquishing certain joys on earth to reap graces for the whole world.

Abortion:

> What about the case where a mother simply cannot afford and cannot emotionally handle the child in her womb, for example, a very young woman, unmarried and still in school?

The crux of the abortion issue is human life in the womb, alive, loved by God, and destined to live forever. If brought into the world as God plans, this child will give to the world a face, a voice, and a personality like no other in human history. Who knows what God has in mind for that one life? All we know is that this life, once conceived, is sacred and precious.

Undeniably some pregnancies are unexpected, ill timed, and in conflict with a mother's life situation. Take the case of a thirteen-year-old girl—shocked to learn a child is growing in her womb, afraid to tell her parents, fearful of her boyfriend's reaction, and worried about the future. Compassion, understanding, and love are what this young mother desperately needs.

Pope John Paul II once told a group of pilgrims in Rome:

> The pregnant mother must not be left alone, left alone with her doubts, her difficulties, her temptations. We must stand with her, so that she might have the necessary courage and faith, so that her conscience will not be burdened. . . . Everyone must in a certain way be with

every mother who is to give birth and offer her every possible aid.

The compassion begins with helping a minor pregnant girl work her way through her situation, beginning with helping her understand what may have led to the pregnancy, helping her to appreciate that she is bearing a human child who can contribute much to the world, helping to orient her to a respect for life, possibly something she may never have known or experienced in the way she herself has been treated.

The quick-fix mentality of abortion takes a completely different route. It eliminates the growing, unborn child. When virtually any abortion is performed, this growing child already has a beating heart, a distinctive pattern of brain waves, a recognizably human shape, and even his own set of fingerprints. It is not a matter of Catholic doctrine but of biological certitude that from the moment the chromosomes of the human sperm and the ovum fuse, a new human being with a unique genetic make-up comes into existence. If this individual is aborted, human life is destroyed.

The baby silently developing in the womb of the frightened thirteen-year-old girl is like the one developing in the womb of a mature, happily married woman with the financial, emotional, and spiritual resources to support her child. In both those wombs, despite the dissimilarities, there is heartbeat, movement, growth. The fact is, the two children growing inside the two mothers are equally human, equally valuable, and equally innocent. Wanting or not wanting the child does not determine the child's worth. Every new human life has value in and of itself. Eliminating such a life is a profound and irrevocable violation of the Natural Law.

Pro-choice advocates forget that there are endless waiting lists of people all over the country begging for infants to adopt, people who would treat them with great love and provide both material and spiritual care, while enriching their own lives.

A parish priest once told a packed church during his Sunday

homily that he himself had been an "unwanted" child, that his worn-out mother had suffered an irksome pregnancy during one of the most sweltering summers in Chicago, that he was the eighth child to enter a crowded, troubled household. "But Someone wanted me", he said. "God wanted me—and in time many, many people would want and need me too." He went on to tell of some of the lives he had touched in his role as a parish priest. If not for the time in his mother's womb, if not for her sacrifice, he added, none of this would have been possible.

God has plans and hopes for every unborn life. He told us through the old, holy prophet Isaiah:

> Can a woman forget her nursing child, and have no compassion on the child of her womb? Even if a mother were to forget the child of her womb, I will never forget you. Look, I have carved you on the palms of my hands (Is 49:15–16).

Eternity:

> How can a God who is Love eternally damn any human being, no matter how great his sins? I thought God was all-knowing and merciful.

The Scriptures are liberally dotted with references to damnation, not to frighten believing Christians, but to warn us to take seriously God's laws and live by them. There would not be a place of eternal spiritual punishment were it not for a gift God places in our hands: free will. The moment he gave our first parents free will, he allowed them to choose good or evil. In our own lives, we have choices too. We can abide by God's laws and reap the blessings or we can overstep them and make our own laws and pay the price.

Following God's laws is sometimes difficult, especially when they clash with those of the world at large. But following them is a small price to pay for the salvation of our infinitely precious soul. Remember, God does not send anyone to hell.

People choose their eternity by the way they live their lives on earth. God makes it very clear how to win heaven and how to avoid hell. Our destiny is entirely up to us. God *is* merciful, but he is also just. He desperately wants us to be with him forever—he created us for that—but he can only bring us there with our own cooperation. Without our cooperation, he cannot force our will. So we have to use the free will he entrusted to us with wisdom, strength, courage, and love.

Artificial birth control:

Sexual intimacy in a marriage binds a husband and wife together. Why should that ever be held back?

In the Christian view of marriage, intercourse is one of a couple's greatest means of showing and deepening the love that binds them together. A husband and wife's bodily union is a sign of their oneness of spirit. Every time a married couple generously love each other in and through their sexual powers, there is a mysterious blending of the human and the divine —the human which the spouses give to one another in their physical embrace, and the divine which God gives them by his grace.

But the Christian faith holds that there are two love functions that intercourse is to serve: the unitive and the procreative. In the unitive, love is fostered *between* husband *and* wife; in the procreative, love is communicated *from* both husband and wife *to* their potential offspring.

Christ showed us through his own life that authentic love is always self-giving, self-sacrificing, and generous; and this is the kind of love that married couples are called to practice, not only between themselves, but from themselves—as one flesh —toward the yet unborn and unconceived children whom God may want to bring into this world through them. Indeed, this is part of a marriage's glory.

The Church believes that contraception is sinful because it tries to separate these two built-in qualities of marital intercourse, dividing something which God has placed together in principle. Most would agree that a husband seeking only children from his wife without any thought of expressing love is using her. The same would be true of such a wife. However, a husband or wife who denies the possibility of procreation does the same. Contraception attacks the total gift of a man and woman to each other.

Moreover, some methods of artificial birth control are abortifacient—they kill the newly formed embryo after conception rather than preventing conception—and using any method which destroys a human life after conception is a very serious offense against God.

In cases where important reasons lead a couple to decide that their children should be spaced further apart, the Church does espouse Natural Family Planning methods; recent scientific breakthroughs have made it possible for a couple to determine their fertile time with approximately 99 percent reliability.

These methods do require some abstinence, but couples who use NFP testify that the challenge is well outweighed by the rewards. First, NFP is a cooperative effort; both husband and wife—not just one or the other—share in the responsibility, bringing them closer. Secondly, there is no danger to health. Thirdly, it puts a husband in touch with the intimate cycles of his wife's body, resulting in appreciation and better understanding. Moreover, couples practicing NFP confide that periodic abstinence actually energizes their love life because it creates stronger desire and it makes the lovemaking that is finally shared again even richer and more exciting.

Covenant of marriage:

> We love each other, the sacrament is between our hearts, why do we need a piece of paper to prove anything?

Marriage between Christians is a contract and an institution, but it is also a sacrament. To live together in mutual harmony, free of the formalities of a wedding or spoken commitment in front of a priest or community, may sound enticing to some couples. Perhaps in the back of their minds they envision a long life of unbroken compatibility and security.

But any one who has entwined his life very closely with another person will know that faults and friction are mixed with the joys. The edge that the sacramentally married couple has over the cohabitating lovebirds is the grace of God! One reason Christ elevated marriage to a sacrament is that the family is such a critical and powerful part of his plan for humanity. Good, happy marriages are an invaluable part of his kingdom because so much truth, goodness, joy, and love can flow from the parents to their children, to other families, to the Church at large. Without the grace of the sacrament, though, and without the blessings of the priest who witnesses the marriage, the challenges to a strong, forever faithful, abiding commitment are much greater and more difficult to overcome. Grace is very powerful, and the happiest and most successful couples marry before God to tap into its rich rewards.

Scripture:

> My Protestant friends know Scripture like the back of their hands, and quote it often. Is it true what they say, that Catholics don't follow Scripture (especially regarding concepts such as papacy, purgatory, and calling priests "father")?

Catholics believe that the source of Christian truth is Scripture and Tradition. We are mindful of the fact that Saint John's Gospel ends with the passage "But there are also many other things which Jesus did; were every one of them to be written I suppose that the world itself would not contain the books that would be written" (Jn 21:25). We know that Jesus said he would send the Holy Spirit to teach us all things.

Scripture is in need of authoritative interpretation because it must be related to the changing circumstances of different eras. Except for Saint Francis there are very few if any Christians who have even tried to follow all the words of Christ literally. How many Protestants do you know carry no money and have only one change of clothing!

The very writings of Scripture would not have been preserved without the following of the traditions of the living members of the Church with Peter at the head. Note, on the papacy, how the dispute between Peter and Paul about circumcision and other aspects of the Jewish law was decided in council with Peter at the head (see Acts 11).

Praying for the dead, which presupposes that they are neither eternally fixed in hell or heaven but must be in some between place where our prayers might help them, is mentioned in the book of Maccabees (a book not accepted by Protestants) and also follows from the way the walls between heaven and earth were broken down by the Resurrection of Christ.

Jesus told the disciples to call no man father (Mt 23:9) to avoid an exaggerated obedience to merely humanly inspired teachings of his time. Note that this could not have been interpreted literally even in early times of the Church since the author of the Acts speaks of Abraham and David as our fathers and Paul refers to himself as a father to his disciples (Philemon 10).

Many Marian doctrines spring from deep meditation and tradition based on Scripture passages such as "Hail Mary, full of grace", for being full of grace precludes the results of the Fall, including death.

To give careful, reflective answers to the claims of those who reject Catholic teaching it is important to have a good catechism on hand such as *The Catholic Catechism* by John Hardon, S.J., *Fundamentals of Catholicism* by Kenneth Baker, S.J., and others listed in the bibliography.

Loving one's enemy:

How does this jibe with standing up for yourself and your rights?

Jesus taught us to love our neighbors, to turn the other cheek if one assaults us, and to put others first. "Blessed are the meek," he told us, "for they shall inherit the earth."

Jesus pointed out that even the non-believers and the evil-doers were kind to relatives and friends, so there is no merit in that; it is natural. The merit comes when we love our enemies, those who persecute or hurt us, or hurt those we care about.

It is important to consider the meaning of the word 'love' in these passages. Jesus does not say 'like', he does not say 'agree with', he does not say 'seek the company of'. When he asked us to love our enemies, he meant that we see past their sins and errors to the person underneath who is made in the image of God. He told us to hate the sin but love the sinner. One example of how we can accomplish this seemingly difficult task is to pray for the person in the silence of our hearts.

Jesus showed us another side of charity, however, when he swept the money-changers from the Temple in a burst of anger. In that situation, he was protecting his Father's house and communicating his message with clear, non-negotiable terms. You might say he was standing up for himself and his rights. He was safeguarding the truth. He was fighting for something he believed in and loved.

Even so, like Jesus and his first twelve Apostles, we are asked to be wise as serpents and gentle as doves, standing up for truths and rights we cherish, but lovingly praying for our opponents as we fight. Jesus taught us that this is possible as he said on the cross, "Father, forgive them, they know not what they do."

Divorce and remarriage:

What is the difference between a divorce and an annulment? What are the exact rules on this and why?

First of all, espousing God's laws in Scripture, the Church holds that two baptized people who contract a valid marriage and have consummated their union by intercourse after marriage cannot be allowed to remarry during the lifetime of their Christian spouse. Moreover, it is the Church's position that there is a permanent bond, until death, in every true marriage.

A divorce is an attempt to dissolve that marriage bond, ending the covenant or contract. It declares that a *valid* marriage is now *broken* by some authority. In fact no valid marriage can be severed by an attempted divorce. Civil divorce actually only regulates the disposition of property and other civil matters. (The Church allows a civil divorce when necessary for the protection of the family, or to ensure their financial support, but does not allow remarriage after the civil severance of a canonically valid marriage.) If no decree of nullity càn be granted, the Church could not bless the individuals' remarriage to other partners. While such a remarriage, civilly, would not result in excommunication, it would bar the remarried Catholic from receiving the Eucharist since the new relationship, in the eyes of the Church, would be one of adultery.

An annulment or—more accurately—a *decree of nullity*, on the other hand, is the Church's declaration that, after proper consideration, a conclusion has been reached that the integral qualities of a valid Christian marriage were lacking to one or both parties to the marriage. In other words, what was taken to be a marriage was actually lacking in some essential characteristics; simply put, *no marriage really existed*. This is why a decree of nullity frees a separated or divorced Catholic to marry again—for, in truth, they are entering Holy Matrimony for the first time.

Some examples of grounds for a decree of nullity are the following conditions existing at the time of the marriage: the deliberate intention never to have children, homosexuality, impotence, *extreme* immaturity, or a forced marriage.

Catholic marriage tribunals carry out an important mission. An annulment process is not a work of mercy, but a work of justice.

Prayer—unanswered:

> How do I answer my daughter who has never received
> any kind of answer to a very important prayer and her
> faith is being tested?

Sometimes the most important prayers appear to go unanswered. For example, a terminally ill person's family
'storms heaven' that he will get better; but he dies. A young
man earnestly asks God to help him get into medical school,
but he is turned away. A single person prays to discover a
soulmate with whom to share her life, but she is alone. Often
the prayers closest to our hearts seem to backfire, and we
wonder if God is listening.

Remember that we have God's word on this: "Whatever
you ask for in my name I will do, so that the Father may be
glorified in the Son. If you ask for anything in my name I will
do it" (Jn 14:13–14). God also says, "Ask and you shall receive,
seek and you shall find, knock and it shall be opened to you"
(Mt 7:7).

I think it is important to remember that we see life one day at
a time, one vantage point at a time. What if the answer to your
prayer would preclude you from getting something much
better? What if God knows you are not ready yet? What if he
intends to give it to you, but wants you to accomplish some
important things for his glory first? God's design for our lives
has been likened to a great tapestry. The back side of it looks
like a ragged, random twist of threads in disarray. Sometimes
our world looks this way. But on the front side of the tapestry
all is ordered and beautiful to the eye. This is what God sees
when he looks down at all our trials and struggles. He promises
to bring good from everything that happens to those he loves.

No prayer goes unanswered. When we give God time, he
finally brings out the surprise he has been holding in his hand
behind his back all along. The important thing is to trust that
he will never let us down.

Unrequited love:

> How does a Christian woman handle the ultimate sorrow
> of a deep love that can never be fulfilled?

Carrying a deep, precious love inside can be the most ecstatic
experience in life. But what about when the person we love
and long for does not love us back? Or what about a person
who does love us back but is not free to marry?

Unrequited love can tear at a person's heart, mostly because
there is no way to express all the generous and noble and sweet
emotions that naturally arise. Perhaps Jesus himself tasted some
of this cruel disappointment in the Garden of Gethsemane the
night before his death.

One important solution is to take the heartache to Christ
and ask him to love and bless the one you love. Pray for the
person, asking that God arrange a path in this life that will
eventually lead him to heaven. Pray for courage in letting go of
him.

Another valuable solution is to channel your love into other
people who need your care. This might take the form of
volunteer work, or helping out an elderly neighbor, or contributing time and energy to a parish ministry. Once the
unrequited lover becomes aware of all the people who do need
love, attention, prayers, and kindness, healing for the lost love
can begin.

Alternate lifestyles (homosexuality, living together instead
of marrying):

> If people choose to live an immoral lifestyle, but do not
> hurt anyone, what's the Church's gripe?

Active homosexuality and living together outside of marriage
are both immoral lifestyles. The Church does not ask that
people refrain from these actions so that bystanders do not get

hurt. The people who get hurt are the ones actually partaking in the relationship.

Sin has a way of dividing people inside. On the one hand, there may be the pleasure and satisfaction of "belonging to someone", perhaps some sense of freedom from traditional bounds. On the other hand, deep inside, anyone with an informed conscience would be wrestling with discomfort.

Aside from the deep-seated psychological toll, sin alienates us from God and finally from each other. Saint Paul proclaimed to the Corinthians (1 Cor 6:9, 10), "Do you not know that the wicked will not inherit the kingdom of God? Do not be deceived: neither the sexually immoral nor idolaters nor adulterers nor male prostitutes nor homosexual offenders . . . will inherit the kingdom of God." Because all sin is essentially selfish, sinful relationships cannot build up the kind of joy, peace, and ultimate fulfillment as will relationships blessed by God.

Therefore, the Church regards sinful living patterns to be dangerous, not because of what they do to others, but because of the unhappiness, disappointment, and havoc they produce in the one who rationalizes it away.

Mixed marriages—intermingling faiths:

How does the Church address young people of different faiths joining their lives and building families?

Mixed marriages have always been a vital concern of the Church, since the family is considered a "living cell" of the Church. In past centuries, Catholics were more separated from people of other Christian denominations or other faiths by community or physical boundaries. Today, with the influx of many religions throughout our society, mixed marriages are more likely to occur. The Church understands and accepts this, with important cautions.

For example, the Catholic man or woman marrying someone of another faith must pledge loyalty to the Church and resolve to protect and cherish its truths. When children come, the Catholic husband or wife is bound in conscience to educate and lead them to understand and follow Christ through the Church.

As long as these conditions are met, a marriage bringing together two faiths might very well be within the providence of God, either because the non-Catholic spouse will discover Christ through the example of the family, or because the married couple is destined to be an image of ecumenical harmony in the "domestic church".

Wayward teenage or adult children:

I loved them, I taught them, I stayed home with them —where did I go wrong?

Every person is created with free will and invited to his own unique relationship to God. In a way, we would like to be able to simply inoculate those dear to us from doubt and sin by some kind of truth and goodness serum, but this is not the way God works.

In our times when there is so little cultural support for a Christian lifestyle it is much more difficult for our young people to follow the teachings of the Church than it was for many of us. God is aware of the evil influences that surround them outside the home, and he will look mercifully upon our children at the time of their repentant return. The witness we have given to the joys of the Faith and the deep peace that we have amidst the many crises of life will give them an indelible impression of what they can return to when the emptiness of their self-chosen life decisions has become too obvious to evade.

Saint Don Bosco, who had a kind of genius for transforming young Italian street thugs into strong, holy men, once said, "In dealing with young people, love is the only key that opens the door." While we must never tolerantly accept our children's sins or act indifferently to their disbelief, it is critical that they believe we unconditionally love them, and that the Father is waiting for the prodigal daughter or son with open arms.

Our agony for them, like Monica's for Augustine, should be transformed into intercessory prayer so that it does not embitter us and render us less able to help our children or others.

Occasions of sin:

> If I join my friends in taking in a movie with explicit sexual encounters, violence or other sinful displays—it's only acting, only a piece of fiction. How does that affect me or my life? I'm not responsible for those acts.

It is true, you are not to blame for anything that happens on the screen; that is the product of a screenwriter, a director and a movie crew. But the danger of viewing violent or unchaste acts is that they can impress our imagination and subtly influence us to do similar things. Films often associate sex and action-packed violence with glamour, suspense, victory, humor, success or rewarding affection, and acclaim. When we begin to rationalize sinful actions because of the possible payoffs they bring, we are being misled.

Naturally, going to a movie and witnessing an action wrong before God does not make us guilty of committing the wrong action. But the Church asks us to avoid the occasions of sin (a person, place, or thing that tempts us to fall into sin) to help us live up to our commitments as friends of Christ.

Young people in particular need to be selective about films, books, and other stories in the media, since they are looking for role models and need to set their faith in real heroes, people who choose to do the right thing even when it might not be lucrative or popular.

A saint who is especially concerned with faith and truth is the newly beatified woman philosopher and Carmelite, Blessed Benedicta of the Cross. Sister Teresa Benedicta of the Cross was the name taken by the famous Jewish convert to Catholicism, Edith Stein, who followed her calling to become a Carmelite nun and was martyred in Auschwitz in 1942.

EDITH STEIN

Edith Stein, the Carmelite whose spiritual peace remained invincible against the terror of Auschwitz, was not always a woman of faith. For many years this gifted intellectual was an atheist, disregarding the notion of God altogether and judging religion a stumbling block to the rational quest for truth. But her desire for truth was so genuine and wholehearted that once she discovered him who *is* the Truth, she embraced him and never looked back.

Prophetically—since she would ultimately lay down her life for her beloved people—she came into the world on the Jewish Day of Atonement, October 12, 1891. The youngest of six in a devout Jewish family, Edith was quick and precocious. By the time she was four years old her older brother had taught her to recite from memory lists of German literary works and their authors. She was eager to learn from the moment she could listen and talk.

The death of Edith's father when she was only two had a significant impact on her childhood. Frau Auguste Stein, her widowed mother, was forced to alter her household and singlehandedly assume the responsibilities of the family lumber business. She picked up the business so quickly and thoroughly that others in the same field, predominantly men, respected her as a master among themselves.

Edith, very much her mother's daughter, grew up with the sharp mind and loving spirit of her Jewish mother. Like Frau Stein, who quietly passed money to the poor, to fellow businessmen in trouble, or to relatives down on luck, Edith subconsciously soaked up the art of giving without expecting in return.

This grace of self-sacrifice would eventually rise to proportions her mother could not understand when Edith later renounced academic acclaim for the cloister and an escape to freedom for a torturous martyrdom to redeem her people.

As a girl of nineteen, Edith as yet had no conception of the value of suffering and the central role it would play in her life. She entered the University of Breslau, majoring in philosophy. Both the pursuit of doctoral studies and the attraction to philosophy set her apart as a rare woman. Edith's choice of fields was related to her lifelong yearning to discover and possess the truth. Edith had already waived hope of finding it in the realm of religion. Her belief in a personal God gradually vanished, though she went through the motions of practicing Judaism out of sensitivity to her devout mother.

Her philosophical studies, the real anchor of her life, led her to the work of Dr. Edmund Husserl, an exceptional German-Jewish philosopher who taught at the University of Goettingen. Edith found this professor so exhilarating and illuminating that she uprooted from the University of Breslau to enroll at Goettingen herself. The relationship between professor and student quickly became a rare and loved blessing to both of them. Husserl was so impressed with Edith Stein that, after she passed her examinations and earned her doctorate in 1916, he appointed her to be his personal teaching assistant and charged her with putting in order his reams of writing. Edith stayed immersed in this task until 1919 when, not being able to secure a real teaching position of her own, she packed and went home to Breslau.

Two unusual episodes happened to Edith which had no relation to each other, and yet fused together to spark a great fire in Edith's mind. Both of the events mysteriously brought her back home to the door of faith. The first occurred when Dr. Husserl sent her to represent him at the funeral of a friend and colleague, Professor Adolf Reinach. Reinach had been killed at the front in 1917. Edith had personally known the man for four years and was quite heartsick to think of his annihilation in battle. He had been a young man in his early thirties with a lovely and devoted wife. This couple had been very warm and gracious to Edith during her years of study. The thought of encountering Adolf's bereaved wife was too upsetting for Edith to bear, mostly because she could think of no consolation to offer the woman.

"Frau Reinach", she later said, "became a consolation to us instead of our being a consolation to her." This curious peace of heart intrigued Edith because it flew in the face of all reason. Frau Reinach shared her secret strength with Edith, saying that it was her Christian faith that held her up and gave her hope. Her belief in eternity, in God's mercy and everlasting love, promised that Adolf indeed still lived! "I accept fully in my heart that Adolf now lives with God. He has reached his goal", she said. The year before Adolf's death, the Reinachs had been baptized in the Lutheran church, and now this woman's belief in the Resurrection and triumph of the Cross gave her a rich and hopeful perspective on her suffering. Naturally, the young widow was deeply grieved, but Edith recognized a joy alongside the grief that touched the deepest part of her soul.

On a second occasion, Edith was on vacation at the farm of dear friends. One night, before going to bed, she picked up a copy of the autobiography of the great Saint Teresa of Avila. Teresa's candid and welcoming account of her own search for truth caught at Edith's heart. She stayed up all night reading it, savoring passage after passage. The message that Christ is the way, the truth, and the life, and that we can live in union with him, sounded the same chord in her soul that the widow of Adolf Reinach did. When morning came, Edith laid down the book and said to herself, "This is it, I have found the truth."

Edith decided to embrace Christianity and was baptized on New Year's Day, 1922. She chose Teresa as her baptismal name. Despite the glorious and quiet joy that filled her, Edith had a pang of sharp sadness later that spring when she broke the news to her mother. Her mother's grief over Edith's conversion lasted throughout Frau Stein's lifetime. However, interestingly enough, years later when Edith renewed her Carmelite vows, her mother, far from her, died at the precise instant. "When I renewed my vows", Edith told her Carmelite sisters, "my mother was with me. I distinctly felt her presence." This gives us great hope that those people whom we love on earth—but must disagree with on matters of faith or love for God—will see and share the truth with us in eternity.

Up until the time that Edith entered Carmel, she made prayer the center of her activity. Her intellectual gifts bore fruit in the Church while she remained active—teaching, lecturing on women's issues, conversing, and writing. She told the women of Germany to take their proper role in the Church and society: "Our nation needs us women," she insisted, "not because of what we have; it needs what we are."

In 1933 Hitler seized Germany, changing the face of Jewish life drastically. Anti-Semitism was rampant in the Muenster area. During this frightening situation, so full of violence and erratic danger, Edith made a holy hour in the Carmelite convent in Cologne. The holy hour centered on the agony of Christ in Gethsemane. She remembered the words of Pascal, the French philosopher: "Jesus is in agony until the end of the world." Edith felt a strange longing to unite herself wholly with Christ in Gethsemane. Her love for her Jewish sisters and brothers was so intense that she conceived the thought of offering herself for them, even as Christ offered himself for us.

At forty-two years of age, a doctor of philosophy and famous lecturer and writer, Edith became a postulant with the Carmelites in Cologne. On April 15, 1934, Carmelite superiors gave Edith formal permission to be clothed in the full religious habit. She took the name Sister Benedicta of the Cross. Her entrance into this world was the beginning of her promise to suffer with Jesus for her people so that they might rise to a new and more blessed life.

A faithful friend of Edith's at this time (Hedwig Conrad-Martius) used to visit her and said:

> Edith always had something childlike and friendly about her. But the feeling of being sheltered and the inner bliss which she reached were, if I may say so, enchanting.

As the black shadow of war covered Europe, Edith—one Catholic Jewess among her sisters—was taken to a convent in Holland for safety. There was talk of moving her out of Europe altogether, but Edith would not be parted from the tragedy of her people. She wanted to be one with them, even to the point of offering her life.

Holland would have been a safe place, but the bishops in that region wrote a powerful treatise denouncing Hitler's inhuman ways of war. The Nazi regime lashed back by scouring the Dutch convents and churches for Jewish converts, particularly priests and nuns.

Edith braced herself for what was inevitable. On August 2, 1942, at five in the afternoon, two SS men came and knocked on the door of the Carmelite convent in Echt. Edith, with her blood sister Rosa, calmly followed the men, their small suitcases in hand, and bade farewell to the weeping sisters. Edith was full of peace and dignity. During her two years in hiding in Echt, she had written a beautiful treatise on mystical theology, "Science of the Cross", in which she wrote: "The Crucified demands that we should follow him . . . that he who formed himself had permitted himself to be formed into the image of the Cross Bearer."

Edith was taken by the Gestapo to Westerbok, Holland, an assembly point for transportation to the concentration camps in the East. Her appearance made one eyewitness, who lived to tell the story, think of "a Pieta without Christ". Another woman recalled that Sister Benedicta "amazed all of us by her quietness and calm".

It is said that she moved about the women and children and tended them, helping and soothing their sorrow and fear.

On August 7, 1942, Edith, Rosa and 1200 others left for Auschwitz. Two days later they were martyred. An eyewitness that recognized Edith standing by the train before leaving Holland forever remembers her unconcealed love and strength as she called out in a steady, clear voice, "Give my love to the Sisters of Magdalena, I am traveling Eastward!"

The integrity and beauty of Edith Stein, Sister Benedicta, shine even more brightly after death. Beatified in the summer of 1987, she remains alive forever—not only in the heavenly kingdom of love and light, but here on earth wherever her story is told.

Hope

Reading letters from Marian Women about their lives and what gives them hope has been an experience of hope for me. I would like to share with you some of their writings here:

> *Woman* who has learned to drink from the well of the Living God. Who does not question how God can do it but trusts her life and the treasure of her life to the Living God who directs and initiates her ways.
>
> *She* hears his voice—she finds out who she is and knows her worth—she is free of jealousy, fear, worry, anxiety —the well is deep within her and she draws from it daily.

Hope is high in her; excitement and joy are evident.

She knows the source of her power and she is not afraid to let go and trust in his ways, not her ways.

She is not afraid to see those around her suffer.

She trusts God to turn the suffering into good.

She has given up manipulating and handling people's lives.

She receives gifts from God and knows her worth so she doesn't drain or demand too much of others.

She is love and she can love, not with human love but with the love God pours into her.

Her peace and joy bubble up from within.

She is free and she sets those around her free,
She is blessed and many are blessed by her.
She is joy, peace, love, patience, gentleness, meekness, long-suffering.

She is broken bread and poured out wine for the hungry that come to her.

She is God's woman!
Her worth is in her being.

The drabness of self-pity with its consequent physical and spiritual energies going down the drain, the well-worn drain of self!

Eulalia McCormick

And these two contributions are from our chaplain, Msgr. Thomas O'Sullivan:

During the persecution the Church underwent in Mexico, the Holy Father visited several priests who told him that the Church in Mexico was through, it was being destroyed by the anticlerics. The Holy Father replied, "If we priests have not been able to destroy the Church in two thousand years, they won't be able to do it either."

Years ago at the Eucharistic Congress in Chicago, an American priest questioned the Nuncio presiding over the Congress concerning how the Church would survive the politics of that day. The Nuncio replied, "When Mussolini was young, the Church was very, very old, and when he is an old man, the Church will still be young."

Letter to my Lord
(by a woman close to death)

Dearest Father, I'm so tired; take me home
   to sleep awhile
and then to wake to a friendly smile.

Let me see the loving eyes, of mother, sisters,
   those I prize
more valuable than earthly things.
Let me mount the golden stair, to see my loved ones
   waiting there.
Let me know the joy reunion brings.

I do not want to leave behind, the ones I hold
   so close and dear,
But I will still be by their side, and always,
   always, hold them near.
Then they will join me when you say, and we will
   be so close once more;
But take me now, please dearest Lord, take me
   through a cottage door.

Colleen Stalla
July 25, 1985

JOAN OF ARC

Joan, the daughter of Jacques d'Arc, was born in the darkest hour of medieval France. Years later, as a young maid, she was singlehandedly to blaze the trail for France's miraculous recovery and rebirth, and then—at nineteen—to be shockingly burned alive in a public marketplace as a heretic and witch. Hers is a story of patriotism, courage, boldness, but above all, trust in God.

Joan is universally acclaimed as patroness of France, but she is equally the special patroness of anyone who seeks to influence the political sphere with the values of faith, anyone who withstands injustice for the sake of truth, anyone who fights impossible odds to achieve what is good and right.

Her story begins in 1412 in the humble farming village of Domremy, France. Appropriately enough, the day of Joan's birth was January 6, the celebration of Epiphany, the feast of the Three Kings. Joan did not appear especially gifted in her early years. She blended in with all the other children in their chores and play. But one day when she was about thirteen years old Joan heard something, and that's when the drama of her gifted life began.

She began to hear voices, often seeing a bright light, and sometimes a vision. As time went on, she identified the voices as belonging to Saint Michael the Archangel, Saint Margaret, and Saint Catherine. Through these voices, God told Joan that she had been born to save France. The voices told her of great victories to come—not to be afraid, for God would be with her.

The import of this message must have stunned young Joan because France had been buried in hopeless warfare for nearly a full century. The Hundred Years War pitting the English and their Burgundian allies against France had resulted in an ongoing blood bath and a vast ravaging of the countryside. Her people were despondent because they were on the brink of losing their homeland altogether and becoming a colony of

England. And she, a thirteen-year-old girl, would awaken France from this nightmare?

For a long time, Joan told no one, but when she was sixteen, the voices directed her to divulge her secret mission and to visit a cousin and his wife who lived in a nearby village. As Joan spoke of the plan to rescue France, her cousin reacted with a healthy skepticism which finally gave way to fascination and interest; he introduced her to Robert de Baudricourt, an official who commanded the country's forces at Valcoeurs on the eastern front.

Commander Baudricourt alternately ignored Joan and made coarse jokes about her. But eventually, after months of her persistence, he, too, admitted a spark of fascination—and he entrusted Joan to two good knights who escorted her on the dangerous eleven-day horseback ride across the wintry backroads of France. At last they reached the towering stone castle of Chinon, home of the Dauphin.

The Dauphin was frequently spoken of by Joan's voices. He was the rightful heir to the French throne, son of the insane King Charles VI; but after his father's death, young Charles VII, twenty-six years old, had forfeited the throne with all its responsibilities for a frivolous life of pleasure. The voices had told Joan that the Dauphin must be crowned king to strengthen the country of France.

But upon arrival inside the castle walls, Joan was taunted and told to go home. To understand fully what Joan was up against, we have only to imagine the skepticism which would block any sixteen-year-old girl today from accessing the President or a Prime Minister in order to steer the course of national events. Multiply that by the rigid fifteenth-century mentality of a woman's place in the world.

But a sudden crisis worked in Joan's favor. Orleans—the city that was the key to the Loire Valley and the gateway to the entire south of France—was abruptly besieged and in danger

of collapse. The King's council, desperate, resolved to hear
Joan out. That evening, by the light of torches, Joan was
escorted into the great hall of the castle with some 300 nobles
of the court. It was a spectacular moment in European history,
a moment which modern day France still exalts.

In marched Joan, a startling sight with her hair short like a
boy's, and her sturdy men's attire—a look she had adopted for
protection on the journey. By way of trickery, Charles the
Dauphin did not wear his princely clothes or sit on his throne;
nor did he greet her. He dressed in ordinary clothes and
mingled in the thick of the crowd. He gloated over the confusion the young illiterate peasant would feel when she entered
the magnificent hall, took in all the lofty, richly-clad guests—
then couldn't distinguish who it was she had come to see.

But he was dealing with a far superior person. Joan—never
flustered by higher ranks—walked purposely right through
the crowd and confronted Charles face to face. She bowed in
homage and declared, "Gentle Dauphin, I am Joan the Maid.
God has sent me to you to help you and your kingdom. You
shall be anointed and crowned in the city of Rheims and you
shall be the lieutenant of the King of Heaven who is the King of
France."

Charles responded that he was not the Dauphin, to which
Joan courteously but firmly contradicted him: "In God's name
gentle Sire, you are."

Amazed but unconvinced, Charles pulled Joan aside to
question her, but *she* took the initiative, whispering in his
ear his own deepest, unshared secrets, thoughts, and fears
hidden even from his confessor. Only God could give her
that knowledge, admitted the Dauphin—but others raised
questions: Was she deluded by the devil? Was she a witch?

The next day Charles ordered Joan to Poitiers to be cross-
examined by a score of learned theologians. During the course
of that investigation, Joan made four prophecies about France,
all of which came true in time. Scholarly men marveled at her

common sense, piety, and wit, and especially her purity of intention—her sole aim to answer her God-given command, then return in peace to her quiet country life. The consensus of the prelates was unanimous: Joan was telling the truth!

An army was quickly reassembled in hopes of lifting the eight month siege of Orleans. Always following her voices, Joan insisted that all the soldiers first go to confession and that all the prostitutes be left behind. She also told the men to take heart, for the King of Heaven was on their side. Some of the generals and knights who left for battle side by side with Joan first balked at a female leader, but in spite of their grumbling, Joan, in gleaming armor, inspired them brilliantly as no one had ever done. The English forts encircling Orleans fell like dominoes as Joan led the way.

When the army finally came in sight of Orleans, Joan was rushed by a ring of soldiers through the one safe route into the city, as the English had barricaded the city only on three sides. Word of the holy warrior-maid had spread and the towns-people were ecstatic; she rode through the streets on her horse to deafening cheers.

At Joan's insistence, no fighting began until a diplomatic appeal was made to the English for a truce. Begging to avoid more bloodshed, she sent the English commander a letter, beseeching his surrender. After three days of silence, she herself appeared on the battlements and shouted out to the English to make peace. The English only spat at her and called her names; the next morning Joan waved high her banner with its inscription "Jesu, Marie", cried "March on!", and led the assault.

Finally electrified with real leadership and hope, the French troops inside Orleans burst into battle. Still, the more adept English were the far greater force. After four days of setback, the French decided to retreat. Joan, flooded with confidence, bandaged up an arrow wound in her shoulder, returned to battle, and mustered all the vitality she could to rouse the

French troops to endure. Her aura of mystic energy inspired the troops to achieve a miraculous turnaround and final victory. They defeated the English and lifted the siege of Orleans.

The crowds of Orleans hugged each other in the streets, singing and crying with joy. All the church bells gloriously rang out. From that day on Joan would be hailed far and wide as the Maid of Orleans. Still following her voices, she planned to intensify this victory with the immediate crowning of the Dauphin at Rheims cathedral.

The cowardly, irresolute Charles dragged his feet, however, explaining that the towns en route to Rheims were still enemy-held, and too perilous for him to travel. With that, Joan hurriedly set out to retrieve those towns by storm, claiming a chain of victories at all the key cities in eight days' time.

One of these towns was Beauvais. In conquering the English at Beauvais, Joan unknowingly dissolved the bishopric and possessions of a Bishop Pierre Cauchon. This Cauchon—a worldly prelate who had served the English side for a handsome price—would later come back to haunt Joan with his vengeance.

But at this point there was only exuberance for Joan as she anticipated the great coronation in the cathedral at Rheims. At last the glorious day came when, amid all the riches of medieval pageantry, Joan witnessed Charles VII finally accept his rightful throne before a jubilant throng. France had its king. And the end of the Hundred Years War was in sight.

But after the coronation King Charles VII still did not act very kingly. Foolishly, he signed a temporary truce with the Burgundians, the English allies; this tied Joan's hands and kept her from completing the victory. Meanwhile the enemy, as Joan had warned the king, used the interval to fortify their troops and entrench themselves more deeply on French soil.

By the time the truce expired, and Joan was again free to march, the Burgundians were ready. At the infamous battle of Compiegne in May, 1430, the Burgundians were so terrifying that the French ran for refuge in a French-held fort. Joan followed but, as she looked up, she realized in horror that her men were hoisting up the drawbridge without her; she had accidentally been left outside. The Duke of Burgundy quickly captured her and imprisoned her in a high tower.

In medieval times, when an illustrious person was held captive, most enemies would honor a ransom, so Joan expected her King to pay her way out. Shockingly, the ungrateful Charles was silent, ignoring his heroine and leaving her to her own fate. Joan tried jumping from her window, but she was only recaptured and sold to the English for a profit.

The betrayal and martyrdom awaiting Joan were based on envy, greed, and malice. The English—enraged by her re-spiriting of the French people—decided to try her as a witch and heretic before a Church court. The "court" was chaired by none other than the hateful French Bishop Cauchon whom Joan had inadvertently ousted in Beauvais. He took his role with delighted relish.

Cauchon also staffed a huge jury with prelates who either feared him or shared his bias. Once the "trial" began, he illegally denied Joan counsel. He also saw to it that the young woman wore chains and irons on her wrists and ankles at all times. Then he orchestrated the bullying of Joan; his cross-examiners tried legal tricks of every kind to break her, hour after hour, day after day, for many months. Added to this, they threatened her with torture, violated her personal privacy with the round-the-clock presence of coarse English guards, and denied her the consolation of the sacraments.

According to the detailed, copious trial records that were preserved and passed down to us, Joan was a sturdy witness in the face of intimidation. When asked whether the voice of Saint Margaret spoke to her in English, she countered, "Why should she speak English? She is not on the English side." When asked whether Saint Michael appeared to her naked, she answered, "Do you think God has not the wherewithal to clothe him?" Several times she warned the bishop, "You say that you are my judge; consider well what you do; for in truth I am sent from God, and you are putting yourself in great peril."

Joan won so much sympathy from the public that Cauchon finally moved the trial to the privacy of her prison cell. Cauchon handpicked the judges who shared his hatred of Joan. Still, Joan was invincible in spirit—promising that her voices were from heaven, that they predicted French victory and a future peace. Finally, Cauchon spewed the verdict from the private meetings to his public: Joan's voices were diabolical, she was a blasphemer. The English secular court was summoned to state her sentence: burning at the stake.

On the day of Joan's execution, as during the days she was on trial for her life, her voices clearly told her to keep strong, God was with her. Joan knelt and prayed aloud for her enemies. A sympathetic English soldier took two small pieces of wood, formed a cross, and reached it up to her. She took it before climbing the scaffold to the stake. Another sympathizer ran to a nearby church for a crucifix which he held up to Joan as the torches lit her stake. Except for the crackling of the fire, there was utter silence. Then, it is recorded that Joan's face was upturned in rapture as though someone were speaking to her and showing her something. "Ah," she cried out, "my Voices did not deceive me!" Moments later she called out "Jesu! Jesu!" and died.

Not long after Joan's death, the Hundred Years War ended and a great peace, like the benediction of God, washed over the land.

Here are some favorite passages about another kind of hope, hope for victory over death:

> *We* do not die inwardly, but only outwardly, inwardly we shall always be what we have always been.
>
> Charles Rich

After a life in which we take and take, we eventually come up against something which we cannot take; death takes us. Hence death is a giving and we should practice by giving, letting go.

David Stendl-Rast

Death would have no great terrors for us if we had a quiet conscience, would it? Why not keep clear of sin, instead of running away from death?

Thomas à Kempis

Death is a birthday.

H. P. Liddon

Death is the soul finding an exit.

Saul Bellow

Death is a sort of moving day—the only trouble with it being the inconveniences. Still, God will one day condemn the house we now live in, so we will have to move to a new residence in the state of glory.

Charles Rich

The world is not an inn but a hospital.

Thomas Browne

To a true lover the halting confession of his beloved is more dear than the most beautiful poem . . . human agony is beyond all an act of love.

Bernanos describing
the death of a priest

God keeps us in this world until it becomes absolutely clear to us that what we are looking for cannot be found in it.

He, Christ, is eternity.

Saint Bernard

Death is ecstasy.

Teresa of Avila

Love

In the famous passage about the gifts of the Holy Spirit, Saint Paul proclaims "and the greatest of these is love" (1 Cor 13:13).

Abbot Damasus Winzen, O.S.B., of Mount Saviour Monastery in upstate New York, who baptized me when I was twenty-one, used to say that the vocation of woman was to be a blessing of love. Saint Thérèse of Lisieux, after spending much time pondering what she could do in the Church, concluded that her part was "to be love".

I would like to challenge you to consider different types of love and to ask yourself which areas of love you need to be more grateful for and which others you need to develop in order to be prepared for the kingdom of perfect eternal love God offers to us if we have let grace open our hearts wide enough. Pray about the areas that need work and thank God for those which he has blessed you with.

The Greeks had four words for love: *storge*, *philia*, *eros*, and *agape*. *Storge* was the familial bond between people—relatives, comrades, workers. Some of these people we have mixed feelings about. For example, you might have a member of the family about whom you habitually report: "I love him, but I don't like him." What can that mean? It signifies that there is a deep bond, maybe even an unbreakable one, but not the sense of delight we often have in the next type of love called *philia*. *Philia*, friendship love, is a love caused by liking each other and having similar values and interests. It is usually free of duty and of strain, a relaxed contentment. *Eros* is passionate love, not only for human lovers but also for beauty, truth, and even God himself. It is the type of love that involves the greatest anguish when it is frustrated, but is a foretaste of heaven when it is fulfilled even for a short time. *Agape* is what the Bible calls loving-kindness. It issues forth in good deeds and crosses all boundaries, for we can care about the welfare even of an enemy though we may never have *philia* or *storge* or *eros* love for such a one.

In his famous book *The Four Loves*, C. S. Lewis describes these types of love and explains how much they need grace to be sanctified. Without God's love, storge love can become fierce and ruthless (as in our family against the world); philia love can lead to cliques; eros love can degenerate into idol worship; and agapic love can smother and nag.

God's love for us and ours for him include all these types of love. We are bonded with God in his family. He is our best friend. We long passionately to be fulfilled by him, and, as depicted in devotion to the Sacred Heart, he longs for us and suffers when we ignore him. God is eager to give us good things, and we show our agapic love for him in terms of the kingdom by our corporal and spiritual works of mercy. Mary and the women saints are models of generous and womanly love for us to imitate in order to love God more perfectly.

Perhaps you would like to tuck into this book favorite passages about love that have inspired you. One of mine is a poem of Gerard Manley Hopkins, "God's Grandeur":

> Though the last lights
>   off the black West went
> Oh, morning, at the brown
>   brink eastward, springs—
> Because the Holy Ghost over
>   the bent
> World broods with warm
>   breast and with ah!
>   bright wings.

FRANCES XAVIER CABRINI

If Mother Cabrini's girlhood dreams had ever been realized, the dreams of many others would have been lost. Cabrini relieves us with historical proof that when God locks the door we want, he always unlatches another—and usually one much greater.

Francesca Cabrini, as she was christened on the day of her birth in 1850 in Lombardy, Italy, might easily have been an inconspicuous nun in an Italian convent. She begged entry into two of them and was bitterly disappointed to be twice rejected on grounds of poor health. The superiors took one look at her and decided she was too frail and might tire too easily.

The dramatic irony is that Francesca turned around and founded an order of her own, opened up sixty-seven charitable institutions around the world, and became one of the most indefatiguable missionaries the Church has ever seen.

She is best remembered for compassionate and brilliant

work among the Italian immigrants in the United States. Pope Leo XIII himself asked her to go west to America after she had singlehandedly turned an Italian orphanage into a novitiate in her twenties, then launched a network of sisters in Italy doing corporal and spiritual works of mercy.

She arrived in New York when she was thirty-nine years old. A clergyman had extended an invitation. He was confused when he saw her and seven of her sisters, for he had written them back and asked them not to come. He suggested they take the next ship home. Francesca refused, secured a place for young orphans, and kept it alive by begging from door to door in the Italian district along Mott Street.

One of Mother Cabrini's secrets of success arose out of her tender embrace of things that first looked impossible. She was indifferent to the caliber of the women she accepted as sisters. She actually wrote to the convent school where she had been educated asking for the overflow of any novices who they did not consider up to their standard. She was never afraid to take a chance on people; she was confident she could make something of them—just as she had turned her earliest group of forlorn orphans in Italy into a happy, capable community of nuns.

Mother Cabrini also had an almost magic calm about money. She used the money when she had it; when she did not, she plunged ahead anyway assuming it was on its way. Trust of that magnitude won miraculous favors for the Missionary Sisters of the Sacred Heart. When one of the sisters reported, for example, that a wine merchant refused to sell them any more wine until they had paid him the forty lire they owed, Francesca told the messenger to look in his pocket. The messenger's pocket, which had been empty, was unaccountably filled with forty lire, neither more nor less. When other supplies were exhausted—milk, bread—those who fretted about it were told to look again; sure enough, milk and bread appeared in the cupboards that had been bare.

This loaves-and-fishes mentality extended to the houses of charity that Mother Cabrini raised from scratch. She did not just channel her energies in New York, but branched out in all directions. She took sisters to Nicaragua, opened a school for children in Grenada, and originated a mission to the Indians.

She opened several schools in Argentina, riding to that country from Chile on muleback across the Andes. After Spanish speaking teachers came to her through the kindness of Queen Maria Christina of Spain, she opened a special school for the daughters of grandees in Madrid. In the Rue Dumont d'Urville, near the Etoile, she opened a boarding house for women. And in the English Southward diocese, she opened another orphanage.

Crossing the Atlantic back and forth twenty-five times, Mother Cabrini always returned to America as her base. In Chicago and New York she began to minister to the prisoners, particularly those under sentence of death. If she could not go to them herself, she always sent someone in her place to comfort them.

In Colorado, she opened a mission for the Italian miners, going down into the shafts with them and sometimes walking as much as two miles in underground tunnels to follow them with encouraging conversation. She set up a makeshift chapel in their camp where they could receive the sacraments in between the difficult shifts of work.

She was always pushing quickly ahead. Some complained that the enlargement of her work was rash and impetuous, but she was a shrewd businesswoman and a great believer. Sometimes she had to make do with almost nothing—as when a couple of vacant stores in Newark served as a school and a warehouse as another school in the Bronx. But for the most part, money would mysteriously pass into her hands and her ideas became realities.

Orphanages and schools were a special love of Mother

Cabrini's, but the heart of her work, finally, was in hospitals. In 1891 she was begged to take command of a small, mismanaged hospital in New York on 109th Street; even with her efforts, the building went into foreclosure, and the hospital was stripped of patients and goods. Mother Cabrini, having witnessed how much good a hospital can accomplish, decided to found an Italian hospital, appealing to Archbishop Corrigan of the area for funds. He gave her fifty dollars, then sent her to four other men who each, in turn, chipped in fifty dollars. With that small sum, she rented a house on East Twelfth Street, bought second-hand beds, made the mattresses herself, bought food at a cheap restaurant nearby and warmed it on a little cook stove, and got to work. One by one, people started contributing their talents, goods and gifts—surgical instruments, linens, loaves of bread—and the sisters who had no nursing experience whatsoever, and who had started with two hundred and fifty dollars, began a medical and spiritual enterprise at Columbus Hospital whose legacy survives to this day. In fact, before her death, Mother Cabrini designed the modern day Columbus Hospital in New York on East Nineteenth Street.

A close friend and advisor once warned Francesca Cabrini not to make a laughing stock of herself, not to assume the weight of the world. "Are you mad?" he asked, "You should leave this sort of thing to the saints!"

But Mother Cabrini was fueled by such a bright flame of love that she did not care what anyone thought of her surprising zig-zagging of the globe. She once wrote in her retreat notes: "Oh Jesus, I love you very much. . . . Give me a heart as big as the universe. . . . Tell me what you wish that I do, and do with me as you will."

In the poor and the sick of the slums, in the dying, in the imprisoned, in the abandoned, Mother Cabrini saw Christ himself. She taught her sisters not to be ethereal and cautious, but to be bold and trusting; not to hide love like a light under a bushel, but to shine it brightly before others. In performing that living action of love, Mother Cabrini bathed the wounds of Christ and brought light and beauty to the world.

The Glorious Mysteries
of the Rosary

1. *The Resurrection:* Jesus rises from the dead on Easter Sunday, glorious and immortal, as he had predicted (Mt 28:1–7).

2. *The Ascension:* Jesus ascends into heaven forty days after his Resurrection to sit at the right hand of God the Father (Lk 24:50–51).

3. *The Descent of the Holy Spirit:* Jesus sends the Holy Spirit in the form of fiery tongues on his Apostles and disciples (Acts 2:2–4).

4. *The Assumption:* Mary's soul returns to God and her glorified body is taken up into heaven and reunited with her soul.

5. *The Coronation:* Mary is crowned as Queen of heaven and earth, Queen of angels and saints.

Meditation on the Glorious Mysteries of the Rosary is recommended for Wednesdays; Saturdays; and for Sundays during Easter, Christmas, and ordinary time.

Afterword

At the end of this book, dedicated to Holy Mary our Mother, we place this, our final prayer:

Dear Mother Mary, I hear you chant this lullaby to me:

Come to me, daughter of Eve,
Seek shelter under my wings.
Let my mothering envelop you.
Become yourself mother to others, then;
Be not forever nurtured, but nurture.
And bring the children of your love
   through your motherhood
To the Mother Church.
And together, as mothers and mothered,
Giving and receiving, receiving and giving,
Each to oneself and others in their proper time,
You, your children, and Mother Church will journey
   to the kingdom
Of heaven, with Mother, as mothers.

If, during the course of reading this book, God has tugged on your heartstrings, if you have been stirred by its content, by all means stop and listen to what he has to say. If he has given you sorrow for your sins, you should respond by seeking out a priest for the sacrament of confession. If he has given you a deeper longing to draw closer to him, then try to give him more of your time —especially by attending Mass more often or visiting him in the Blessed Sacrament. If he has given you food for thought, then meditate on these things that you may grow in wisdom. If he has given you peace in your heart, then thank him and rejoice in his abundant blessings. In any case bow your head to his greatness and ask Mary, your Mother, to draw you ever closer to him through his Holy Catholic Church.

Bibliography

Marriage

Dennehy, Raymond, ed. *Christian Married Love*. San Francisco: Ignatius Press, 1981.

Hogan, Fr. Richard M., and LeVoir, Fr. John M. *Covenant of Love: Pope John Paul II on Sexuality, Marriage, and Family in the Modern World*. New York: Doubleday, 1986.

Pope John Paul II. *Familiaris Consortio*, 1981. (This and other Church documents can be obtained from Daughters of Saint Paul: 50 St. Paul's Ave. Boston, Mass. 02130.)

von Hildebrand, Dietrich. *Marriage*. Manchester, New Hampshire: Sophia Press, 1984.

Motherhood

Driscoll, Pat. Pat is co-founder of *Womanity* and author of many beautifully illustrated leaflets, booklets, and cards about chastity, and also celebrating maternity under the patronage of our Lady. (Write to *Womanity*, 2141 Youngs Valley Rd., Walnut Creek, Ca. 94596.)

Feeney, Leonard. *Elizabeth Seton*. New York: America Press, 1938.

Melville, Annabelle. *Elizabeth Bayley Seton*. New York: Charles Scribner's Sons, 1951.

On Being a Single Woman

Muto, Susan. *Celebrating the Single Life: A Spirituality for Single Persons in Today's World*. New York: Doubleday, 1982.

Pope Paul VI. *Humanae Vitae*. San Francisco: Ignatius Press, 1978.

On Being a Consecrated Woman

Avila, Teresa of. *The Interior Castle*. Tr. Allison Peers. New York: Image Books, 1961.

Avila, Teresa of. *The Life of St. Teresa of Avila*, Tr. David Lewis. Westminster, Maryland: The Newman Press, 1962.

Dubay, Thomas, S.M. *". . . And You Are Christ's"*, *The Charism of Virginity and the Celibate Life*. San Francisco: Ignatius, 1987.

Manteau-Bonamy, H. M., O.P. *The Immaculate Conception and the Holy Spirit*, Teachings of Maximilian Kolbe. Kenosha, Wisc.: Prow Books, 1977.

von Speyr, Adrienne. *The Christian State of Life*. San Francisco: Ignatius Press, 1986.

von Speyr, Adrienne. *They Followed His Call*. San Francisco: Ignatius Press, 1986.

Enjoying Our Feminine Traits

Chervin, Ronda. *Feminine, Free, and Faithful*. San Francisco: Ignatius Press, 1987.

Sister Geneviève of the Holy Face. *A Memoir of My Sister, St. Thérèse*. New York: P. J. Kennedy and Sons, 1959.

Jamart, Rev. François, O.C.D. *Complete Spiritual Doctrine of St. Thérèse of Lisieux*. New York: Alba House, 1961.

Lisieux, Thérèse of. *Story of a Soul*. Tr. John Clarke, O.C.D. Washington, D.C.: ICS Publications, Institute of Carmelite Studies, 1976.

St. Thérèse of Lisieux: Her Last Conversations. Tr. John Clarke, O.C.D. Washington, D.C.: ICS Publications, 1977.

The Joyful Mysteries of the Rosary

von Balthasar, Hans Urs. *The Threefold Garland*. San Francisco: Ignatius Press, 1982.

von Speyr, Adrienne. *Handmaid of the Lord*. San Francisco: Ignatius Press, 1985.

Wright, John J. Cardinal. *Mary Our Hope*. San Francisco: Ignatius Press, 1984.

The Sufferings of the Body

Benedek, Therese. *Psychosexual Functions in Women*. New York: Ronald Press, 1952.

Deeken, Rev. Alfons. *Growing Old and How to Cope with It*. San Francisco: Ignatius Press, 1986.

Donahue, Lois. *Dear Moses . . . Letters to Saints and Other Prominent People*. Huntington, Ind.: Our Sunday Visitor, 1984.

Grumbine, Deborah. *How to be Happy and Holy in Your Own Home*. Rockford, Ill.: Tan Books, 1988.

The Sufferings of the Heart

Chervin, Ronda. "The Working Mother: To Be or Not to Be". Liguori Pamphlets, Liguori, Mo. 63057.

Esway, Judy. "Measure by Love". *Prayers for Working Mothers*. Mystic, Conn.: Twenty-Third, 1985.

Linn, Dennis and Matthew. *Healing of Memories*. New York: Paulist Press, 1974.

Linn, Dennis and Matthew, and Fabricant, Sheila. *Healing Life's Greatest Hurt*. New York: Paulist Press, 1985.

Healing Our Feminine Faults

Capua, Father Raymond. *The Life of Saint Catherine of Siena*. New York: P.J. Kennedy and Sons, 1960.

Chervin, Ronda. *Workshop Tapes*. Pecos Benedictine Monastery, Pecos, New Mexico 87552.

de Monfort, Louis Marie. *True Devotion to the Blessed Virgin Mary*. Bay Shore, New York: Montfort Publications, 1985.

Siena, Catherine of. *The Dialogue*. Tr. Suzanne Noffke, O.P. New York: Paulist Press, 1980.

The Sorrowful Mysteries of the Rosary

Ratzinger, Joseph Cardinal. *Behold the Pierced One*. San Francisco: Ignatius Press, 1986.

von Speyr, Adrienne. *The Cross: Word and Sacrament*. San Francisco: Ignatius Press, 1983.

Wright, John J. Cardinal. *Words in Pain*. San Francisco: Ignatius Press, 1986.

On Being a Woman of the Church

Bouyer, Louis. *Woman in the Church*. San Francisco: Ignatius Press, 1980.

Buckley, Cornelius, S.J. *Your Word, O Lord . . . , Meditations for College Students—and Anyone Else*. San Francisco: Ignatius Press, 1987.

de Lubac, Henri Cardinal. *The Motherhood of the Church*. San Francisco: Ignatius Press, 1983.

Pope John Paul II. *Redemptor Hominis*, 1979. (This and other papal encyclicals can be obtained from Daughters of Saint Paul. See address on p. 259.)

Ratzinger, Joseph Cardinal. *Seek That Which Is Above*. San Francisco: Ignatius Press, 1986.

von Speyr, Adrienne. *Three Women and the Lord*. San Francisco: Ignatius Press, 1986.

The Sacraments of the Church

de Lubac, Henri Cardinal. *The Splendor of the Church*. San Francisco: Ignatius Press, 1986.

The Prayer of the Church

Chervin, Ronda, and Neill, Sister Mary. *Bringing the Mother with You: Healing Meditations on the Mysteries of Mary*. New York: Seabury Press, 1982.

Kempis, Thomas à. *The Imitation of Christ*. Milwaukee: Bruce, 1940.

Scriptural Rosary. Chicago: Scriptural Rosary Center, 6 North Michigan Ave., Chicago 2, Ill., 1961.

Catholic Faith, Hope, and Love

Baker, Kenneth, S.J. *Fundamentals of Catholicism* (3 vol.). San Francisco: Ignatius Press, 1982–1983.

Derrick, Christopher. *That Strange Divine Sea*. San Francisco: Ignatius Press, 1983.

The German Bishops. *The Church's Confession of Faith*. San Francisco: Ignatius Press, 1987.

Hardon, John, S.J. *The Catholic Catechism*. Garden City, New York: Doubleday, 1975.

Keating, Karl. *Catholicism and Fundamentalism*. San Francisco: Ignatius Press, 1988.

Larkin, Francis, SS.CC. *Understanding the Heart*. San Francisco: Ignatius Press, 1980.

Lewis, C. S. *The Four Loves*. New York: Harcourt, Brace, Jovanovich, 1960.

Pieper, Joseph. *On Hope*. San Francisco: Ignatius Press, 1986.

Pope John Paul II. *Redemptoris Mater*. Published with commentary in the book *Mary, God's Yes to Man*. San Francisco: Ignatius Press, 1988.

von Balthasar, Hans Urs. *Heart of the World*. San Francisco: Ignatius Press, 1980.

The Glorious Mysteries of the Rosary

von Speyr, Adrienne. *The Gates of Eternal Life*. San Francisco: Ignatius Press, 1983.

Wright, John Cardinal. *Mary Our Hope*. San Francisco: Ignatius Press, 1984.

Women Saints

Baldwin, Anne B. *Catherine of Siena*. Huntington, Indiana: Our Sunday Visitor Press, 1987.

The Collected Works of Edith Stein. Ed. Dr. L. Gelber and

Romaeus Leuven, O.C.D. Washington, D.C.: ICS Publications, 1987.

The Collected Works of St. Teresa of Avila (3 vol.). Tr. Kieran Kavanaugh and Otilio Rodriguez. Washington, D.C.: ICS Publications, 1976–1985.

Cristiani, Msgr. Leon. *Joan of Arc—Virgin-Soldier*. Boston: St. Paul Editions, 1977.

Dirvin, Joseph I., C.M. *Mrs. Seton: Foundress of the American Sisters of Charity*. New York: Farrar, Straus, and Cudahy, 1962.

Gorres, Ida Friederike. *The Hidden Face: A Study of St. Thérèse of Lisieux*. U.S.A.: Pantheon Books, Inc., 1959.

Herbstrith, Waltraub. *Edith Stein*. San Francisco: Harper and Row, 1971.

Hutchinson, Gloria. *Six Ways to Pray from Six Great Saints*. U.S.A.: St. Anthony Messenger Press, 1982.

Kalberer, Augustine, O.S.B. *Lives of the Saints: Daily Readings*. Chicago: Franciscan Herald Press, 1983.

Keyes, F. P. *The Sublime Shepherdess*, The Life of Bernadette of Lourdes. New York: Messner, 1940.

Lorit, Sergio C. *Frances Cabrini*. New York: New City Press, 1975.

Tylenda, Joseph N., S.J. *Portraits in American Sanctity*. Chicago: Franciscan Herald Press, 1982.

Valentine, Mary Hester. *Saints for Contemporary Women*. Chicago: The Thomas More Press, 1987.

Index

Women Saints

consecrated women: Teresa of Avila, 54

faith: Edith Stein, 230

healing of faults: Catherine of Siena, 154

hope: Joan of Arc, 238

love: Frances Xavier Cabrini, 249

motherhood: Elizabeth Bayley Seton, 28

overcoming temptation: Mary Magdalen, 170

single women: Kateri Tekakwitha, 43

suffering of the body: Germaine of Pibrac, 112

suffering of the heart: Margaret of Castello, 123

sweetness: Thérèse of Lisieux, 67

Prayers

Act of Consecration, 36

Litany of the Blessed Virgin, 200

The Magnificat, 199

The Memorare, 35

Our Mother Prayer, 199

A Prayer for Healing, 127

Prayer for Marian Women in Ministry, 208

Prayers for Priests, 183, 184

Prayers for unborn children, 137

The Rosary, 197ff.

Stations of the Cross, 103

Answers about
the Catholic Faith

Topics

Abortion, 216

Alternate lifestyles, 226

Artificial birth control, 219

Celibacy and virginity, 215

Chastity before marriage, 214

Confession, 211

Divorce and remarriage, 223

Eternity, 218

Loving one's enemy, 222

Marriage, 220

Mixed marriages, 227

Occasions of sin, 229

Ordination of women, 212

Scripture, 221

Sunday Mass, 209

Unanswered prayer, 225

Unrequited love, 226

Wayward children, 228

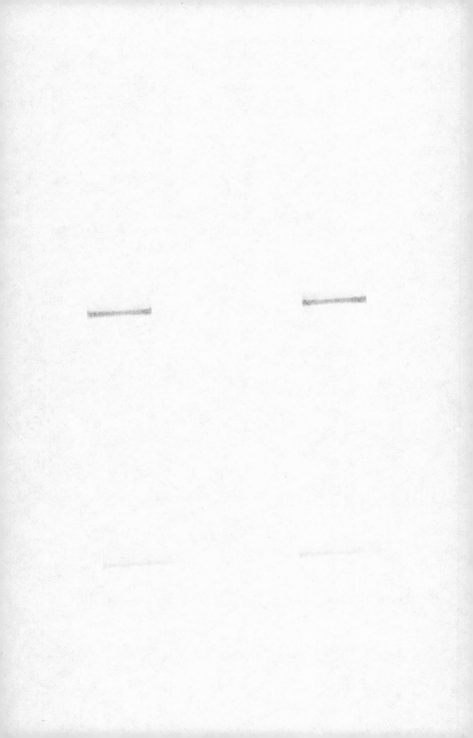